CW01584264

bath

the insider's guide

introduction

Bath (make sure you pronounce it Barth, northerners) is packed with history, architecture and foreign language students. Not to mention plenty of bars, pubs and clubs to destroy those cultured brain cells. Let itchy Bath be your guide to all things entertainment, grab a bottle of Mr Matey and jump on in.

The views expressed in this publication are those of the authors and contributors and are not necessarily those held by the editors or publishers. Readers are advised to form their own opinions and we welcome any contributions. All details, listings, addresses, phone numbers are correct to our knowledge at the time of going to print. itchy Ltd cannot be held responsible for any breach of copyright arising from the supply of artwork from advertisers.

© itchy Ltd
Globe Quay
Globe Road
Leeds
LS11 5QG
t: 0113 246 0440 f: 0113 246 0550
e: all@itchymedia.co.uk
www.itchycity.com

ISBN 1-903753-03-1

City Manager: Richard Gingell Editorial Team: Simon Gray, Ruby Quince, Mike Waugh, Andrew Wood Design: Matt Wood, Tony Ward, Steve Wiseman Cover Design: artscience.net Maps: Steve Cox at Crumb Eye Design Contributors: Katie Monk, Kelly Halborg
Jamie Oliver pictures copyright David Loftus

GOJobsite™

THIS BOOK HAS THE BEST PLACES TO SPEND YOUR MONEY.

WE HAVE THE BEST PLACES TO MAKE MORE MONEY.

We have hundreds of thousands of new jobs every month from Europe's leading companies. You could find your dream job in seconds, and you might soon need an Itchy Guide to New York, Paris, Sydney...

www.gojobsite.co.uk

contents

THE INDEPENDENT

THE INDEPENDENT ON SUNDAY

why not subscribe and

save over 60%

For a limited period only, The Independent would like to offer you the chance to purchase The Independent & Independent on Sunday for only £1.50 a week, with our advanced purchase payment subscription. Payments can be made by simply telephoning

0800 783 1920

quoting REFERENCE IS01000ITCHY

Offices open Mon to Fri 9am - 9pm, Sat & Sun 10am - 4pm

Answer machine at all other times.

When the application has been processed - which may take up to three weeks - The Independent will send you your fully pre-paid vouchers, which can be redeemed at any news outlet. Alternatively, if you prefer home delivery, please let us know the details of your local participating newsagent (including address and postcode) and we can organise the rest! Your newsagent may charge a nominal fee for this service.

foreword

Jamie Oliver

These itchy guides are fantastic. When it comes to travelling, be it social or business, there's so little time to decide where to go and what to do. I spend half my life darting around all over the place, so when I'm visiting cities that I've never been to before, I like to cut to the chase and get to the right places. The itchy guides are just what I've been looking for.

These guides will definitely help you get the most out of a trip to a new city, and whether it's a two hour visit, a night on the town or a long weekend, the itchy team will push you in the right direction. From where you can find the most cutting-edge R'n'B to the coolest threads, as well as some good grub, a few drinks and maybe have a bit of a boogie. And at long last, someone's cottoned on to the fact that once in a while a dodgy pub and a bit of karaoke beats posing at the latest bar opening, hands down.

It's reassuring to know that the itchy team take their research seriously. I know from experience that they certainly know how to mix business with pleasure.

– Jamie Oliver

itchycity.co.uk

For what's happening right here, right now and in 17 other cities... www.itchycity.co.uk. All the events, all the time, with news on gigs, cinema, restaurants, clubs and more. You can sign up for updates on anything from hip-hop to happy hours, vent your anger about our reviews and get discounts for your favourite venues. Whatever's happening in the city, itchycity's there.

And for when you're out, we've made that hulking great big wap-phone actually useful. Next time it's 1am and you're gasping for a Guinness, whip out the wap and find your nearest late bar... **wap.itchycity.co.uk**

American

Firehouse Restaurant

2 John Street - 482070

My mouth is watering just writing about the food here. Maybe it's because I'm Northern but if you don't get fed to busting at a restaurant then what's the point of eating there? You won't walk away from here with that feeling I can assure you. Gorgeous pizzas, lamb, chicken, puddings, wine and if there is a party of you, get booked into the room upstairs. If you're lucky you'll have the place to yourselves, and it feels like your own private dining club, plus you can make as much noise as you like. Tremendous fun.

Chargrilled Rack of Lamb £13.95
House Wine £10.95

English

Browns

Orange Grove - 461199

Chain bars eh? You take an old crumbling high street bank, post office or what have you, stick a bit of new furniture in, a dash of paint, a kitchen sink and away you go. Luckily Brown's have managed to do something a bit special with this old police and fire station. I didn't spot the fireman's pole but the old cell doors are still there. The building was still being used until recently so some unsuspecting old lag might just spot their name in the graffiti which still adorns the doors. There's no draught beer but a good selection of bottled lagers to choose from, along with wine and cocktails.

Steak, Mushroom and Guinness Pie £7.95. House Wine £9.95.

Café Retro

18 York Street - 339347

Constantly busy with lots of chatter from the clientele. Successfully achieves the ambience of good continental cafés. Not always easy to get a table or the eye of one the waiters to get you one. A good place to catch up on local events posted on the wall at the back of the café. Good fry ups, burgers and chips as well as other wholesome foods.

Lamb Kleftico £13.00. HW £8.50.

Circus Restaurant

34 Brock Street - 318918

They say location, location, location are the watch words for buying property, so why the Circus Restaurant ended up in Brock Street is anyone's guess. The food is great, but it can be a touch on the

BROWNS™

RESTAURANT & BAR

ORANGE GROVE · BATH BA1 1LP

TELEPHONE: 01225 461 199

FULL MENU ALWAYS AVAILABLE

CHILDREN'S MENU

EXTENSIVE OUTSIDE DINING

COCKTAILS · BEERS · WINES

PRIVATE DINING ROOM

SEPARATE MEZZANINE BAR

BOOKINGS TAKEN

OPENING TIMES

11.00am-11.30 pm Monday-Saturday

12 noon-11.30pm Sunday & Bank Holidays

expensive side and service can veer towards the slow, especially when ordering drinks.

Baked breast of chicken stuffed with banana on a coconut curry cream sauce, £12.75. House Wine £12.75.

The Hole in the Wall

16 George Street - 425242

One of the doyens of Bath eateries has just undergone a millennium makeover, but it was hard to see what was wrong with it in the first place. At the pricier end of the market, but well worth a visit. Birthdays, Christenings, Bar Mitzvahs - you know what I mean.

Slow Braised Shank of Lamb £14
House Wine £12.50

Hullabaloos

36 Broad Street - 443323

Even though the name sounds like something out of The Jungle Book, Hullabaloos isn't an animal-infested cartoon restaurant where you get served by a bunch of talking monkeys, more's the pity. Unfortunately the monkeys are usually big groups who take advantage of the BYO policy to see if they can drink eight bottles of Blue Nun each. If you can put up with the crowds (and they're not frequently bad) it's also a pretty good place to go as a couple; the food's excellent and well presented, there are a decent selection of veggie dishes and a good three-course deal as well. Even when there was 15 of us the food didn't take long to arrive and when you eventually run out of your own booze (eight bottles of Blue Nun is not enough for a real man) they'll sell you some more from their cellar.

Braised Lamb £12

The Moody Goose

7a Kingsmead Square - 466688

A restaurant that doesn't hang its Michelin star around its neck like a medallion on a hairy chest. For good measure there are two AA rosettes awarded as well. Not for one minute should you think that makes it pretentious though. Reflecting the fact that such awards have been bestowed the restaurant affords you, the diner, a rewarding experience with friendly, knowledgeable staff, who have that true talent of making you feel special without being annoying.

Roast Local Partridge £17 HW £11.15

TOP FIVE...

Places to impress a date

1. **Firehouse Rotisserie**
2. **Circus Restaurant**
3. **Hole in the Wall**
4. **The George Inn**
5. **The Ring O'Bells**

The Moon and Sixpence

6a Broad Street - 460962

An old favourite amongst many locals for eating or just sharing a bottle with friends after a hard days shopping. If you are just drinking, it's nice to tuck yourself away inside the door in the corner, but if you're eating try to avoid sitting upstairs (unless in a big group) where the loos and kitchens are, as you'll have a constant stream of people tramping past you all night. Great food served in a buzzing atmosphere.

Roast Pheasant £13.50 HW £9.70

No.5 Bistro

5 Argyle Street - 444499

Excellent bistro where all the food is cooked to order. One of those restaurants that easily lives up to its reputation. Even though the restaurant is smoke-free

you can always nip outside for a fag if you're desperate, but chances are you won't want to leave the gorgeous surroundings. They even have BYO on Monday and Tuesday evenings, nice people that they are.

Chargrilled Loin of Lamb £13.85

House Wine £9.95

Olive Tree Restaurant

Russel Street - 447928

No smoking. So if you can hang out long enough without any gaspers, and your wallet can withstand the pace then give the Olive Tree a pop. It's certainly not cheap (whole grilled Cornish lobster with fresh herbs and cream £19.75), but the food is especially good. If you can't handle the no smoking policy, it's not unheard of for people to nip upstairs to the hotel for a crafty woodbine, but you didn't hear that here.

Grilled Loin of Venison £17.25

House Wine £12.50

French

Beaujolais Restaurant

5 Chapel Row, Off Queen Square

423417

Stylish French restaurant with a cheeky, slightly saucy, edge to it. Opened in the early 70's, this restaurant has been serving decent French food to knowledgeable locals for years, easily earning its reputation as the best French restaurant in the city. Slightly on the expensive side,

Get cheap meal offers sent to your phone.
wap.itchycity.co.uk

but with affordable three course lunch and dinner deals. You'll be hard pressed to find anything as good as this this side of the English Channel. If the weather's good try and bag a table in the walled garden out the back. Oh, and if you ask for cream with your dessert keep an eye on what it's poured from.

Fillet of Beef £16.95. HW £11.80

Café Rene

Unit 2 Shires Yard - 447147

Smashing little French café tucked into a quiet corner of Shires Yard. If it wasn't for the crap weather so often associated with Bath it would be just like being on holiday. Outside heaters and great baguettes.

Chicken Curry £5.25

Café Rouge

Gascoyne House

Upper Borough Walls - 480042

Despite being part of a successful chain with all the trappings which have probably been mass produced at the same firm who fit out the Irish theme pubs, it's not actually that bad. Expect to find a mixture of coffee swigging locals and office people having a swift 'meeting' during the day.

Lemon Chicken £7.95. HW £9.60

Clos du Roy

1 Seven Dials - 444450

Recently voted 'Best Fine Dining' in a Bath restaurant survey. This is nouvelle cuisine done well, but in my opinion I'm afraid it does tend to lack atmosphere and feels a little too formal, especially when the pianist is tinkling away on a Friday or Saturday evening. Save it for those special occasions.

Rack of Lamb £17.50 HW £9.95

Rendez Vous Provencal

2 Margarets Buildings - 310064

Slightly out of the way French restaurant, which if you can persuade yourself to walk this far will reward you with some fine Provencal cuisine.

Mon-Wed 2 course meal £14

Rack of Lamb £15 House Wine £10

Tilleys Bistro

3 North Parade Passage - 484200

I don't think bistros will ever go out of fashion when there are places like this. Not your average menu - when the evening comes around all you get is starters. But starters with a difference. Basically you choose what you want and help yourself. A big favourite with the

THE INDEPENDENT The best writers, the sharpest opinions

Gemma
21
Accountancy student

Where do you tot up your tequilas?
Rat & Parrot
And for the odd meal out?
Shangri La
You look like a million roubles.
Where do you shop to dress?
Maze
What fuels your passion in Bath?
By the end of the night, I've forgotten
And what drives you to drink?
Parking drives me nuts in the town centre

locals, who obviously know what they're doing.

Scallops in White Wine £7.50
House Wine £10.90

Woods

9-13 Alfred Street - 314812

It's like having a meal at your mum's

house. Except now, your mum has developed some frighteningly good culinary talents. And she's got more rooms in her house than you remember as a child. And, she's going to bill your ass at the end of your dinner. Anglo/French cuisine, served up with impeccable style and professional service.

Roast Local Partridge £14.95 HW £11

Indian/Asian

Balti House

79 Lower Bristol Road - 330144/448354

BYO balti bliss in a part of town you're more than likely to fly past in your motor having stocked up for the week at Sainsbury's. There can be no doubt that it's a party venue. Since the BYO thing has come over from Oz it's a shame more restaurants don't do the same. It's a good option for filling those quieter evenings early in the week, as the Balti House will testify.

Chicken Korma £3.85. Bring your own booze.

Jamuna

9-10 High Street - 464631

Not immediately obvious from the street, but if you stumble out of Bar One downstairs in search of some decent curry sustenance then step next door, wind your way up the stairs and you're there. One big brightly-lit curry house at your disposal. Only it shuts at midnight so there's just enough time to bolt your biriyani before heading for the taxi rank across the road.

Biriyani £7.75 HW £9.35

Pria Balti

4a Argyle Street - 462323

I'm sure the Pria Balti has given out many a blotting paper balti after a Boater experience across the road. With most dishes under a fiver and a kindly 10% student discount on takeaways, you'll be feeling really glad the next morning that you stopped by. Open 'til 2am on Fridays and Saturdays.

Chicken Biriyani £6.50 HW £7.95

Rajpoot

4 Argyle Street - 466833 / 464758

Not your ten pints of lager and curry here mate. This is proper eating out this is. Restaurant, not curry house. The Rajpoot has an envied reputation for serving the best curries in town. The fact that it won the Indian Restaurant of the Year eight years running means it's talking my kind of language; top-notch curries. But at a price, as it ain't cheap.

Chicken Biriyani £8.75 HW £9.75

Italian

Bella Pasta

15 Milsom Street - 462368

Boring pasta chain serving boring pasta dishes to tourists. I don't know if the chefs are Italian, but if they are they should be ashamed of themselves.

Pollo Cacciatora £8.99
House Wine £8.75.

Caffé Martini

9 George Street - 460818

Spacious restaurant at the top of town serving excellent pasta in hearty portions at reasonable prices, though they don't seem to accommodate large groups very well.

Tagliatelle Campagnola £7.95
House Wine £8.95

Caffé Uno

The Empire
Grand Parade - 461140

Big selection of pasta dishes in a rather grand setting at the Empire. Frescoes on the wall give the impression of a Renaissance Palazzo, well, as near to one as you're going to find this side of Tuscany. Relaxing, attentive (but not annoying) staff and decent Italian fodder.

Pollo al Masala £9.25. HW £9.95

Capetti's Restaurant

12 Argyle Street - 442299

Make Capetti's your first and last experience of Italian in Bath, that is unless you have Italian friends and can eat at their place for free. Three-course lunch £6.90

Penne Disperata £7.50 HW £11.95

RISTORANTE ITALIANO
CAFFE UNO
CAFFÉ UNO
The Only Italian You Need To Know
The Empire, Grand Parade, Bath BA2 4DF
Tel: 01225 461 140
www.caffeuno.co.uk

Il Bottelino

5 Bladud Building - 464861

Great big pizzas, great big atmosphere, but not great big prices. Go there, fill yourself up, and then take a doggy bag. There's usually some sort of office/birthday party going on, which makes it all the more fun to eat there, and the waiters won't take the piss if you try and order in Italian.

Pizza Piccante £7.90 HW £11

Mediterraneo

12 George Street - 429008

One of the best Italian restaurants in Bath - stylish but unpretentious décor, an Italian menu that for once ventures beyond pasta and pizza, and very friendly service. Family-owned, and family friendly.

Pasta Galore

31 Barton Street - 463861

There is a courtyard garden for summer diners, and a log fire to keep you nice and toasty in the winter if you're sitting inside. Beware the rather intrusive wall mirrors, which reflect you stuffing your boat race with pizza. Good honest Italian grub. 2-course lunch £5.50

Tagliatelle con Agnello £.6.40 HW £8.40

Pizza Express

1 Barton Street - 420119

Everyone has their own favourite Pizza Express pizza and mine is American Hot. That's not forgetting the dough balls. Made in true thin crust Italian style with no gimmicks they've just added a few new pizzas into the mixer to start you off all over again. I mean you're going to have to try them. Aren't you? Be rude not to.

American £6.20 House Wine £9.85

Trattoria Cellar Restaurant

39 Gay Street - 427919

Quality Italian like Mama used to make. It makes you wonder how all those 'chainy' pseudo Italian joints stay in business when there are places like this around. I mean why bother when you can get real authentic dishes here? 2-course lunch £6.95, Mon - Sat 12 - 2pm.

King Prawns and Brandy £15.95
House Wine £10.50

Mexican

Las Iguanas

Seven Dials - 336666

If you like schmoozing Latin-American style, you need to suss out Las Iguanas. Especially good value in the summer, as you can eat one, two, or three courses for £4, £5 and £6 respectively (until

find the nearest restaurant on your WAP phone.
wap.itchycity.co.uk

6.30pm). Grab a Pulp cocktail, sit in the courtyard or brightly-coloured restaurant and soak up the lively atmosphere. Try XimXim - Brazilian lime chicken for those not in the know.

Xim Xim £8.50 HW £9.50

Oriental

Fu Hau Chinese Restaurant

27 High Street - 464143/400047

Why is it that there are only two types of restaurants that lend themselves so easily to background music; jazz cafés and Chinese restaurants? Fu Hau is a good case in point. Delicious traditional dishes served to a background of tasteful music. Along with really good service, there's a chance that you may be tempted into trying something that you may not have thought of before. Spot on.

Crispy Chilli Beef £6.80 HW £9.20

Mai Tai (Thai)

6 Pierrepont Street - 445557

Fairly typical Thai restaurant in that you can't go wrong with anything on the menu, as you know you're going to enjoy whatever you order (providing you like Thai food, obviously). Pleasant surroundings, pleasant staff, pleasant prices.

Beef with Cashew £5.80 HW £7.95

Shangri La Restaurant

2 George Street - 338200

You wanna Thai experience without the hefty airfare? Try the family-owned (read 'more likely to please') Shangri La. A large restaurant with tasty, reasonably-priced food served to you by staff wearing traditional costume, which is certainly a better look than the usual white shirt/black clip-on bow tie.

Chicken Green Curry £5.95 HW £9.95

Sukhotai

90a Walcot Street - 462463

If you ever have trouble deciding what you want to eat when you go out to dinner, then perhaps you shouldn't come here. But then again you would be slightly daft if you didn't. There's a rather large menu to get stuck into and it's all good stuff. Even when it's closed the smells from the kitchen are delicious.

Chicken Thai Style £6 HW £9.50

Xian

28 Charles Street - 424917

A whole combination of tastes to be had in one restaurant with a reputation of being the best of its kind in Bath, and who could argue? Another restaurant with a huge mirror down one wall, which is really off putting. I know it's a trick to give the impression of loads of room but if you're an ugly sod like me, how are you going to feel staring at yourself throughout the meal?

Quarter Crispy Duck £9.50 HW £9.95

Others

Baku Wine Bar & Brasserie

7 Argyle Street - 444440

Mellow wine bar with an airy atmosphere and excellent high-backed comfy chairs too, though pity the poor person who has to sit opposite you as their seats are a little on the uncomfy side. Completely revamped since its Maxsons diner days, but the food doesn't seem to have improved much. There's a fairly decent selection of wine to choose from, as you might expect, as well as a fairly decent price tag for a large glass.

Thai marinated tuna with a mango salsa, £7.95. House Wine £10.50

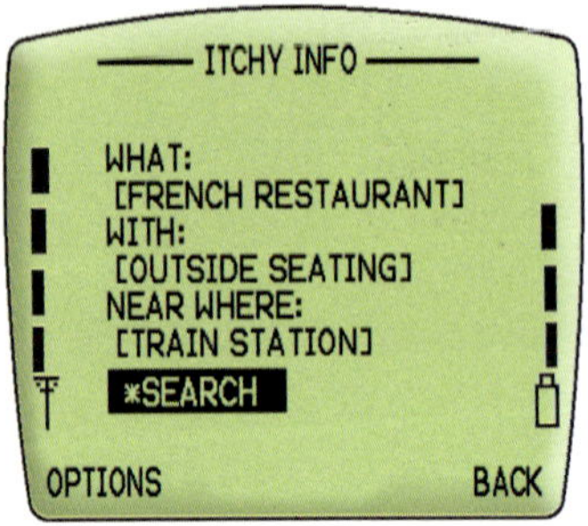

Bathtub Bistro

2 Grove Street - 460593

This used to be a largely vegetarian restaurant with staff who would turn their noses up at you if you ordered meat. That's changed as they now have a comprehensive selection of meat and vegetarian. On Mondays and Tuesday you can BYO.

Spicy marinated jerk chicken with permentoes, tomato and chili, £8.05. Hot. HW £8.95.

Garfunkels at the Empire

Orange Grove - 461465

The sun bleached, flyblown menu in the case outside, which hasn't changed for a few years describes itself as "Pizza & Pasta, Chicken, Steaks, House Specialities, Lunch Specials (Mon - Fri)". So it's all things to all men really. More chain food, but there are kiddies packs to keep you entertained. Try to get the waiter to give you a pack even if you're a big kid. It might take your mind off the food.

Old fashioned Hamburger £4.90
House Wine £9.35

Green Park Brasserie

Green Park Road - 338565

Renowned as much for its live jazz at weekends as its laidback atmosphere and food. Housed in the old Green Park Station building and still retaining some of the original features, this is definitely one to tick off the list and then come back to again and again.

Duck Breast Confit £14.95 HW £8.95

Green Street Seafood Cafe

6 Green Street - 448707

Sprung from the shop below, this restaurant has emerged as one of Bath's lead-

ing lights in the restaurant community. An ever-changing seafood menu featuring uniquely styled dishes. Even the fat Fleet Street hacks have caught up with it, and it's currently the Good Food Guide 2000 'Seafood Restaurant of the Year'.

Zuppa de Passcatori £15.90 HW £9.95

Rascals Bistro

8 Pierrepont Place - 330201

Even though this restaurant has won loads of Les Routiers awards they can't have gone early in the week 'cos it's dead quiet, which makes it seem funny eating there when you're rattling around like a spare part. It's decorated with loads of old film and music posters and things on the walls which serve to remind you how old you are. Best to go at the weekend when it's a whole load livelier.

The Wife of Bath

12 Pierrepont Street - 461745

Near the top of the list for romantic restaurants in Bath. Perfect for first date dinners, as you can tuck yourself up in quiet corners away from the prying eyes of other diners. The food will give you enough to talk about if you're shy.

Pork Dijonnaise £9.80 HW £11.50

TOP FIVE...

Cheap Eats

1. **Il Bottelino**
2. **Pig & Fiddle**
3. **The Porter**
4. **The Green Tree**
5. **Adventure Cafe**

Vegetarian

Demuth's Vegetarian Restaurant

2 North Parade Passage - 446059

The only restaurant in Bath to target committed vegetarians. Serving a varied selection of meals (obviously without meat) including vegan. Even if you're a dyed in the wool meat-eater take one of your veggie friends out for dinner and show them you care, you'll be pleasantly surprised how good food can taste without blood. Leave the ciggies at home, you can't smoke them here.

Medlana Sufi Aubergine £9.75
House Wine £9.75

www.itchybath.co.uk

Scoff's Café

Kingsmead Square - 462483

Wholesome wholemeal food to make you feel like you're doing the right thing. You feel that if your mother wanted you to eat somewhere, it'd probably be here. Stalwarts such as Homity Pie have been served for years, and the place is rarely quiet, which has to be a good sign, doesn't it? Good line in the thickest of stodgy choccy cakes, and if you believe in the pleasure/pain principle, someone's going to die at birth for these.

The Walrus & The Carpenter

28 Barton Street - 314864

Not strictly a vegetarian restaurant (as you can tell from the recommended dish), but they do have a fine veggie

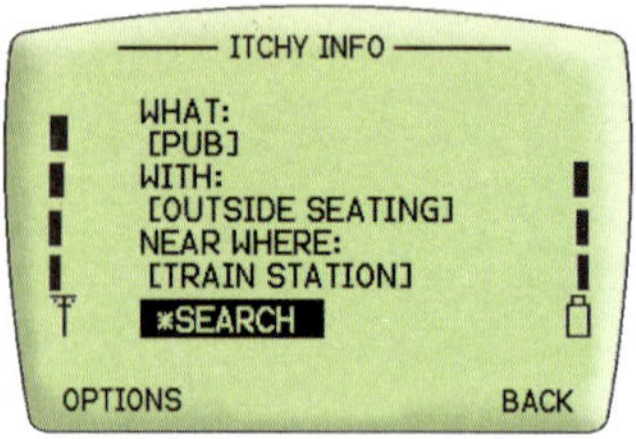

Find what you want using your WAP phone wap.itchybath.co.uk

selection, so we've squeezed them in. If you polled frequent Bath diners for their fave haunts you'd probably hear 'The Walrus' feature highly amongst the replies. OK, so the menu not's going to rock the culinary world, but what it does, it does well. From the outside it looks like one of those places you simply have to eat in, the word 'cosy' was invented for this restaurant.

Quarter Pounder £7.25 HW £9.25

Cafés

Adventure Café

5 Princes Buildings - 462038

Ultra-cool, daytime hang out that does good coffee, and a palatable range of natural foods at reasonable prices. Its position on George St allows you to watch the world go by, either inside looking through the huge shop-like windows or from out on the street. Foods are well prepared and there's a wide selection of sandwiches as well as some decent salad

THE INDEPENDENT The best writers, the sharpest opinions

and nacho dishes. They also make great, freshly-made fruit milkshakes and smoothies. The waitresses are usually dead saucy, service is friendly, and if Kylie Minogue or Johnny Depp were in town you'd probably find them here. However, there's more chance of your fresh herb salad containing chicken and crispy bacon.

Ciabatta with chicken and crispy bacon with a fresh herb salad, £3.75.

No alcohol

Café Soleil

9 Terrace Walk - 445446

Good atmosphere, if you like the sound of 70-year old women nattering about their latest bout of gout. The last conversation I heard here revolved around an old dear's daughters new-found success and lesbianism at university. I mean, really, have these people no shame? There's coffee – not surprising really. Window seats, street views and idle gossip.

Harington's

9 Queen Street - 461728

Mighty fine breakfasts served up in one of Bath's most charming little hotels. It's the attention to details that make the difference – no fingernails, hairs or any other bodily bits or pieces in any of your food. And the orange juice is real juice. Nothing makes my early-morning hangover worse than skanky, watered down, chemical infested orange concentrate.

Full English Breakfast £5.75

Jazz Café

1 Kingsmead Square - 329002

Not to be confused with its London namesake, Jazz Café is laid-back and friendly, but you're more likely to be scoffing on a jacket potato than some unpronounceable potato metaphor. More of an upmarket greasy spoon in the day, but the cosy evening atmosphere draws in the couples.

Jazz Cafe Big Breakfast £5.00

Lovejoys Café

7-10 Bartlett Street - 446322

You may just come across this little hidden gem whilst antique hunting in the Bartlett Street market, but you should seek it out even if you're don't. Sadly, you won't find Ian McShane slobbering over a the full English, but the food is worthy of attention. Breakfasts are big and sumptuous and served at lunchtimes too if you just couldn't manage anything solid in the morning. Loads of other goodies also on offer.

Terrace Restaurant

Jolly's Dept Store - 462811

Conjures up images of continental sophistication, but think more along the lines of monkeys let loose with a spatula. The surroundings are better than the department store would suggest, but the food is a little less appealing. How's your chicken? Rubbery. The pleasant atmosphere should have added to the enjoyment, but unfortunately not.

Get cheap meal offers sent to your phone.
wap.itchycity.co.uk

The Alehouse

1 York Street - 400088

The underground cellar bar was once a perfumery but is now sniffed out by students who enjoy the sweet smell of a good deal. WKD £1.50 a bottle, Carlsberg £1 a bottle, house doubles from £1.85 (double G'n'T £2.05), bottles of Grolsh and Fosters £1.15. The lounge bar is more for the locals and can get packed with rugger buggers on Saturdays.

The Assembly Inn

16-17 Alfred Road - 333639

Since being refurbished a year ago, The Assembly now looks like a real English boozer, complete with a nicotine-colour wash on walls and ceiling. The crowd is a mixed lot, ranging from students and locals to tourists and concert-goers from the nearby Assembly Rooms. Drinks are very good value and if there isn't a specific promotion on pints, 4-pint jugs are usually available from £6. Bottles of wine from a fiver. Food 12-7pm but if you order before close you can take home a something-and-chips for £2.50. Bargain.

The Bath Tap

19 St James's Parade - 404344

Excellent gay pub at the bottom end of town. This is where the Bath gay scene begins and ends. On Thursday there's a Karaoke night, and on Fri and Sat night DJs play chart and handbag (no hard house) until 2am.

FEEL THE PRESENCE
JOSETTE SIMON. ACTOR.
A MELLOW MIX OF SPIRIT AND SOUL.
THAT FLAVOURS WHATEVER IT TOUCHES.
MORGAN'S SPICED
• Try it with ginger beer and lime, mixed with friends.

The Beehive

Lansdown Road - 420274

If you like to hike for your pint then join the swarm of other cider drinkers at The Beehive. They all made the trip, have built their own community and now only need to come out for the dole cheque run. Jukebox free on Sundays 7-close. Cider £1.60 £2.10.

The Bell

MORGAN'S SPICED

103 Walcot Street - 460246

If you want to know where all the festi-val-goers migrate to in winter, then look no further than The Bell. The live music Monday, Wednesday and Sunday

the BOATER

Argyle Street, Bath
01225 464211

- SKY TV
- POOL ROOM UPSTAIRS
- LARGE TREE-LIT BEER GARDEN
- FREDDIE'S OUTDOOR COCKTAIL BAR
- FOOD SERVED 12-3, 7 DAYS A WEEK
- EXCELLENT SUNDAY ROASTS
- RED BULL BAR

lunchtimes keeps those festival fires burning and The Bell even has its own stage at Glastonbury. Rickshaw bikes are made out the back and are used for city tours which cuts on pollution (£7.50 adults £3.50 children over 5). Beer garden/drive gets busy in summer. Veggie rolls available for £1.60. Barnstormer Bath Ale £2 a pint.

The Boater

MORGAN'S SPICED

9 Argyle Street - 464211

A local stamping ground for the Bath Rugby Club, The Boater is a great place to come in summer due to the huge beer garden near the river. Wed and Sat the Red Bull bar opens downstairs, and is largely occupied by the Uni hockey or netball teams getting their money's worth from the £1.50 pints of Fosters. Sky Sports, pool tables upstairs, food 12-3pm. Basket meals from £2.95.

The Brain Surgery

36-37 Dafford Street - 330056

One of those odd front room pubs you

THE INDEPENDENT ON SUNDAY The best coverage of news & sport

find in every city. When approached about a free listing in this book I was told they weren't interested, which makes you wonder what they might have to hide.

Broadley's Wine Vaults

1 Gascoyne Place - 422603

Looking distinctly like a club from the outside, Broadley's is more for local sports lovers than anyone else, and is only open on three monthly contracts. This means it may close at Christmas, not too big a shame. Worth a visit if you're around that neck of the woods between 7-9pm for a £1.50 pint of Fosters or Blackthorn, only with NUS though.

The Crystal Palace

Abbey Green - 424210

Another pub in the competition for Bath's oldest boozer, and at between three and four hundred years old it could very well be in the running. If you were allowed to quaff your beer in the Abbey Green this would be the ideal drinking spot, but you can't, so you'll have to make do with the ample garden at the back. When the sun occasionally bothers to come out, the tables under the shade of the vines are much coveted and jealously guarded, but the rest of the garden has ample shade if you need it. Inside, where the wood panelled walls lurk, expect to be faced with a fine atmosphere created by the healthy mix of tourists and locals. Make sure you enter from the front, and not the side, as this bar has the most room, unless you enjoy rubbing up next to total strangers (actually...). The decent food on offer in the evening deserves sampling.

Coeur de Lion

Northumberland place

As the smallest pub in Bath, The Coeur de Lion is a tourist magnet. With an interesting menu and seating outside all year round in the attractive Northumberland Place, it's a great place to come for time out in a piece of Bath's history. Food 12-2.30pm. Winter Roast £4.95, Summer Ploughman's £4.50. Sunday 8pm close.

The Curfew

11 Cleveland Place West - 424210

Cosy, wood-panelled pub on the edge of town heading out towards the motorway. You can use this pub as both a halfway house when meeting people from that side of town before heading off down Walcot Street, and as an excellent footy venue. Comfortable sofas upstairs arranged in an auditorium style mean teriffic viewing angles for the game. And if the match you're watching doesn't live up to the hype then no one will be offended if you nod off in the corner. A seat near the fireplace downstairs in the winter is well coveted.

Dark Horse

4 Northampton Street - 425944

This gay-friendly pub is situated behind the Royal Crescent at the top of town. Well worth the walk up the hill to get there, although you might not think so halfway up. It used to have a reputation as a smokers' pub, but that's all changed since its makeover and attracts a more health-conscious crowd.

Flan O'Brien's

Westgate Street

Once called Mulligans, Flan O'Brien's has had a bit of a rough trot. However, with the arrival of new management it hopes to compete with the proposed opening of an O'Neills by having a much needed revamp in January. Food is only served until 3pm and is mainly Irish cuisine (lots of spuds). Bantry Bay Mussels £4.95. Ongoing promotions on Guinness. Shots £1.85 with mixer.

The Garrick's Head

8 St. John's Place - 318368

Located next door to the Theatre Royal, many of the clientele here are luvvies. It gets packed in the summer and when shows have just finished. The Garrick's always looks beautiful so it's nice to sit outside on a warm evening sipping a G'n'T, and savouring the last of the summer sun, darling. The Bath Ghost Walk sets off from here as the pub is haunted, apparently. Food 12-3pm Mon-Fri, 12-6pm Sundays. Bath sausage and mash £4.95.

George Inn

High Street
Norton St Philip - 01373 834224

A legendary pub located eight miles outside of Bath in the tiny village of Norton St. Philip, it's definitely one of those country pubs you go to on a first date to impress. Over 700 years old and built by the Carthusian Monks, it's officially the 3rd oldest continuously licensed drinking venue in the country. If you've had too much and cannot drive back home you can book a room for the night, but at £90 (inc. breakfast) for one of the four poster rooms it ain't cheap but is inspiring. With glorious food (traditional English), a large selection of wines and real ales and a large garden to sit and watch the cricket in the summer, there's a fair chance you might submit to a big comfy bed to sleep it off.

The Hat and Feather

The Grapes

14 Westgate Street - 310235

Small and a bit dingy, The Grapes is more of an old man's pub during the day although it does fill up with tourists at lunchtimes. Go on a Friday night and take advantage of the great offers available on bottles which are sometimes given away for free to get you in the door. The food is also good and relatively cheap for Bath. The spicy beanburger and chips is pretty ropey but quite temptingly edible at only £1.49.

The Griffin

Monmouth Street - 420919

This grade II listed building, dating back to 1736 is your archetypal local, it's even got the obligatory ghosts. You will probably spot them sat at the bar, sinking a few beers (slowly) and talking about their past lives. Occasional live music. B&B £17.50 a night. Food 12-3.30pm, Sun 12-4pm (need to book).

Hat and Feather

14 London Street - 425672

Sister pub to The Bell, but much less hip-pyish, The Hat, like Butlins, has got a rigorous line-up of entertainment. Unlike Butlins, however, it's all good adult entertainment. Sunday: Eat My Hat; swingy-dancey-fusionesque music, Tuesday: Film Club upstairs; cult classics for free, Wednesday: DJ Derek, watch the mental little guy work reggae wonders. Also rickshaws available as taxis (tip only), Thursday: Play Group; bring your instru-

ments and have a jam. Apparently where The Propellerheads got together. Friday: Petty Fraud Clinic; hip-hop, break beat, swing and sometimes a live PA or decks. Saturday: Scorchio (upstairs); Latino house, downstairs live bands in autumn/winter. Check out the current ceiling display of trippy sculptures á la management. House wine £5 to take out. Slapper (Navy rum and coke) £1.80.

The Hobgoblin

47 St. James's Parade - 460785

Another favourite with the students, mainly due to the 20% discount (2-8pm) on drinks. The Hobgoblin offers a range of home-cooked food at reasonable prices as well as that culinary masterpiece, the deep-fried Mars bars. Other mouth-watering delights include the array of 30 flavoured vodkas (£2.15 for a double) such as bubble-gum, black jack and dolly mixture for those that like to get pissed while reminiscing about their childhood innocence. Live music on a regular basis. Downstairs room available for hire. Food Mon-Wed 12-2.30, Th-Fri 12-5.30pm, Sat-Sun 12-4pm.

The Huntsman

1 Terrace Walk - 482900

Many find themselves in The Huntsman after the pubs shut, purely and simply because it's open 'til 2am, six days a week and the queue for Po Na Na just isn't worth joining. The place itself isn't anything special, but sadly in this day and age it's a rarity to be able to continue drinking past 11 without going to a club and braving a dance floor. Unfortunately, rarities have their price and you won't be the only one who wants to drink until 2. Get there before 11 at weekends to avoid queuing. Bizarre Bath comedy walks (£4.50/ £4 students) leave here at 8pm every night April-October if you fancy a laugh.

The King's Arms

1 Monmouth Place - 425418

Another age-old local. Dating back to the 1750's, this ex-coaching inn is a great place to come if you want to lose yourself in a smoky atmosphere and emerge as your favourite pop star. The locals (mainly men who probably haven't moved since the pub was built) are good-humoured and unusually don't stare at you like you're a freak when you walk in (unless you're American, of course). You can also take advantage of

FIND THE NEAREST CASHPOINT ON YOUR WAP PHONE
wap.itchycity.co.uk

the B&B facility for £40 a night per double room if you've sunk too much cider. Live music Saturday and Sunday evenings. Doorstep sandwich £1.50. Pint of cider £2.

Lamb and Lion

Lower Borough Walls - 474931

This much-improved pub is now a good place to meet before heading up to the top end of town. The big screen TV shows every major sporting events so avoid it like the plague if you hate raucous males foaming at the mouth with excitement. Thursdays is 121 night with £1 entry and £1.21 for a drink all night and Sundays is free karaoke. The heated beer garden is a bonus any time of year. House Wine £8 a bottle. Food 12-6pm Mon-Sat, 12-5pm Sundays.

McCabe's

Fountain Buildings - 425403

With a decor of colourful kite-like hangings and a pool table in the back room, McCabe's is the place to come if you're a young local skiving off work. An interesting mix of DJ's and Irish music (not all at once), this new bar could spawn quite an intimidating crowd. And I'll bet someone's missing those sheets. Stella £2.40 a pint, spirits from £1.50 without mixer.

TOP FIVE...

Quiz Nights

1. **Tilley's Bistro**
2. **Walrus & Carpenter**
3. **Central Wine Bar**
4. **Paragon Wine Bar**
5. **The Ring O'Bells**

The New Inn

23-24 Monmouth Place - 332643

With its choice of real ales, cider and home-cooked food, the cosy New Inn is hospitable whoever you are. Board games available, but their own 'Ring the Bull' is your best bet for entertainment after a few halves of shandy. Closed every afternoon except Saturday. Pub grub served 12-2pm except Saturday 12-9pm. Steak and Mushroom Pie and Chips £4.20.

The Old Green Tree

Green Street

If you can fit you and a mate in the door then it's actually worth holding your stomach in for. A very small, friendly local which serves food at lunchtimes only.

The Oliver

Green Street - 464666

Definitely one to bring your gran to. Very family friendly with a large bar area, non-smoking restaurant and upstairs games room. The Oliver is well maintained and was the home of the Bath Oliver biscuit (unavailable on premises). Excellent promotions on every night and all major sporting events covered, this is a very inexpensive place to get trolleyed. Children welcome but the young-looking must take ID to be served alcohol. Mon and Wed: £1.29 pint Carling, Tues: Fosters or John Smiths £1 pint with NUS, Thurs-Fri 7-close: Fosters, Carling, Caffreys, Strongbow, Courage Best, house wine and house doubles all £1.65 each.

Pig and Fiddle

2 Saracen Street - 460868

One little piggy went to the flea market...and ended up stopping off for a pint. Or so it looks. A bit crusty around the edges, The Pig is still a good place to sit outside and sample some of the finest meaty chunks such as the Porky's Revenge Fry Up (£4), and wash it all down with one of their six local ales. A popular haunt with students and ageing hippies, it can get busy in summer. Food Mon-Sat 12-6pm, Sun 12-5pm.

The Porter

15 George Street

The Porter was taken over by Moles Club (upstairs) six years ago, and steadily turned it from a scruffy pub into a rather decent pre-club venue serving up excellent vegetarian food (until 9pm), and good sounds via the pubs two sets of Bose speakers. If you want to get away from the general melee of people, then take yourself away into the aptly titled Quiet Room. As well as the upstairs bar, the Cellar Bar has come into its own over the last couple of years as a small live music (Tuesdays and Thursdays) and comedy (Sundays) venue.

Pulteney Arms

37 Daniel Street - 463923

If you like sport then this is the pub for you. Not your big screen theme pub, but a real traditional boozer with knowledgeable locals talking all manner of sports from hockey to football, squash to rowing. Known mostly as a rugby pub, it's best to sample the atmosphere before or after Bath Rugby have played at home at the Rec. There's been a pub here since 1759, and although there are no ghosts

to be had, the warming fire and real gas lanterns will make you feel very cosy in the winter. Especially with one of the huge chip butties or Sunday Yorkshire puds inside you washed down with one of the six real ales. Check out the framed beer certificate from Usher's on the wall. The figures will amaze.

Rat and Parrot

Westgate Street - 461642

You know the score by now with these pseudo-traditional chain pubs - plenty of good deals, plenty of people wanting to consume them. During term-time, pints are £1.50 and Beach Nights all-year round on Friday and Saturday mean that some well-equipped girls go round the pub getting you to splash out on a shot of tequila or a test-tube for £1.50. Very large place to start a very large night. House wine £8.65. Food 12-8.30pm Mon-Thurs, 12-7pm Sat & Sun. Persian lamb casserole £5.95.

The Roundhouse

Cheap Street - 425911

With its ideal location, and interesting architecture it's easy to be drawn in to The Roundhouse, especially if you're new to the area. However, it's probably worth walking a little further and spending your money in a nicer more square building. Restaurant upstairs. Steak and Stilton pie £5.25.

Sam Weller's

Upper Borough Walls - 474911

Another pub hinging its tourist trade on Dickens. Sam Weller was a Dickensian character, for those that are bothered, which obviously Brad Pitt was as he was spotted here having a swifty. Small but central, the floral Sam Weller's is a decent place to drink, has a non-smoking area and sells jugs of Carling for £6 all day, every day. Can't say fairer than that. Quiz night Monday: 50p entry to win gallon of beer/cash. Food 11-9pm Mon-Sat, Sun: 12-6pm. Messy Dog £3.50.

The Saracen's Head

Broad Street - 426518

One of the oldest original pubs in Bath, The Saracen's was where Charles Dickens holed up when he was writing The Pickwick Papers in the 1830's. Due to its wealth of history, tourists tend to flock here to sample the real ale and authentic victuals. Fish and Chips £4.95, pint of John Smiths £2, Fosters £2.15.

The Star

23 Vineyards - 425072

Absolutely steeped in history, The Star is one of 30 National Heritage pubs and popular with anyone who likes their beer served in a jug, the traditional way. The grade II listed building hasn't been altered inside or out during its 260 year history, and it really feels like you are taken back in time when you walk through the door. There's no background music and no machines, so get in there quick before they turn it into a museum. Bass £2, Staropramen £2.40, House doubles £1.95. Take-home cartons available.

Smith Brothers

11 Westgate Buildings - 330470

Despite being refurbished in November '99, the Smith's still pulls in the same crowd; students and wide boys joining forces to get completely mullered, usually when there's a decent game on. The place is fairly spacious and there are pool tables upstairs so it's worth coming, even if you're not one of the lads. Wednesday 6-11pm 241 on selected lines.

The Trinity

James Street West - 400042

Sometimes you wanna go where everybody knows your name. But if you're a stranger to The Trinity no one will care what you're called. A place where the regulars are very regular and the rest of us never return. It might be worth leaving this one until you've bedded yourself in for a few years. Food 12-2.30pm Local Ham and Eggs £3.75. Pint of Flowers £2.

Volunteer Rifleman's Arms

3 New Bond Street - 425210

Tucked down a back alley, The Volunteer's is a strange little place but the staff are always good hosts and it's nice to sit outside and watch the world go by. There's a mixed crowd in the day but it can be quite a gay hangout at night. Pint of Oakhill £2.10. Food served 11-3pm, non smoking dining room upstairs. Beef and Ale pie 'n' chips £4.95.

Bars

All Bar One

High Street - 324021

A fine example of the huge chain of 54 bars dotted throughout the country. It gets away from the usual suits you find in most versions with a good mixture of students, tourists and locals. Expect the customary wine and beer selection as well as good food. With big front windows it's a perfect venue for a brief Saturday afternoon respite from the shopping, but beware once you're drawn in it can be difficult to escape.

Bar Karanga

Manvers Street - 446546

Partly owned by the two Karanga boys

This bar serves as pre-club meeting point for the Karanga nights at Babylon. With loads of space inside and a reasonably sized outside seating area, it can still get quite packed at weekends with a fair proportion of townies on Saturdays. As far as food goes there's a baguette and pannini option during the day with other

stuff in the evenings until 9pm. Unfortunately, there are no plans to become a late bar due to the notoriously fickle nature of the Bath licensing authorities. A bit off the beaten track at the bottom end of town, if you've just come off the train it's about two mins walk from the station - so check it out.

Baty's

The Old Post Office - 331532

Don't bother with Baty's bar if you're a bit short of readies. During the week the suits come in to talk shop, and at the weekend prepare for townies and a middle-aged bunch who still think that denim shirts are an acceptable form of attire. Baty's do, however, organise a salsa class on Thursday evenings if you fancy a bit of Cuban culture but make sure you come after 9.30pm, as it's only £2. For those in denial of their financial status, you can pay by Switch, but prepare a good excuse for the bank manager the next day. Food 11am-11pm. Bus to Evolution in Bristol runs on Saturdays 11pm for £7 return fare and entry.

Browns

Orange Grove - 461199

Once upon a time, this building was a fire station, then it became a police station, and now it's Browns. With such an interesting history and great service, it's easy to see why tourists enjoy the place so much, particularly the downstairs restaurant. At the weekends, a younger crowd frequents the upstairs bar. Take advantage of the 241 offer on cocktails (from £4.35) Mon-Fri and 2 courses for £5.95.

The smoking area out the back was once a police cell. It still has the original tiled walls. HW from £9.50 a bottle. Open 'til 11.30pm 7 days a week.

Central Wine Bar

Upper Borough Walls - 333939

A recent addition to the ever-growing list

of bars in the city centre, and a welcome one at that. It's an ideal spot to stop if you've got a load of bulging bags and you need a pick me up. As is the criteria with any bar these days, the wine list is good, there's a variety of beers on offer, and the food is reasonably priced. Not everyone gets the mix right, but here they seem to have done just that. The atmosphere changes in the evening, but then you'd expect it to.

Ring O'Bells

Widcombe Parade - 448870

What an absolute gem of a place. A regulars bar and a decent restaurant to boot. With a comfy room upstairs you can get away from the rather loud live jazz played there on Tuesday evenings. The Sunday roast is heartily recommended as well. It's just a shame that you get kicked out around 11. Yet another crap statistic of the archaic Bath licensing laws.

Lambretta's

North Parade House - 464650

It's neither Brighton or Rome but it tries. If you can see past the snapping tourists you'll be impressed with the fully kitted out scooter outside. A mod's paradise, the bar also draws in a younger crowd who dig the cool 70's juke box and the personal service. The 18-80 Scooter Club meet here every month. House doubles £2.20, toasties £2.50, bottles of Carling £1.50.

The Litten Tree

23 Milsom St. - 310772

It's well worth the effort of donning full body armour and forging to the bar at The Litten Tree if only for Bar 135 on a Sunday (soon to be Monday) and Thursday 7pm-close, as the entry of £1.35 entitles you to part with only £1.35 for each of your chosen bevvies, and if you tag on the happy hour (4-7pm weekdays) you could have a decent drinking sesh, cheap as chips. For those that haven't had enough by 11pm, a bus runs to and from The Works in Bristol on a Friday and Saturday night for £5 and £6 respectively, including entry fee. Pint of Badger Best £2.15, house doubles from £2.15 without mixer.

Paragon Wine Bar

1a The Paragon - 466212

At top o'town you can get away from the 'townie' boozers, tuck yourself into one of Bath's most atmospheric drinking establishments, enjoy a full on drink before hitting Moles for a bop. Strong continental lager on draught and a good selection of wine. Mainly populated by locals, but it's worth tracking down if you want a good old natter with friends by the fire in the upstairs room. Especially good on Sunday as this is noodles night, big bowls of steaming noodles with loads of different sauces to choose from. Nice venue to hire for intimate birthday parties too.

Pulp

Monmouth Street - 466411

Primarily a cocktail bar and part of Las Iguanas, Pulp is a top spot to come with a few choice friends. With excellent staff and enough drinks to sink a small ship, it's time you took an induction into the 'pulp lifestyle'. Good squishy served all day and the Pulp Burger (£5) is particularly recommended. Thursdays DJ Leroy plays drum'n' bass, house and strictly no cheese. Smoothies from £3, fresh strawberry martini £4, H/W £10.

The Raincheck Bar

34 Monmouth Street - 444770

Perfect coffee? The owner has been sent to Italy to learn how to make coffee by Illy espresso. Good cocktails? The bar man used to have his own cocktail bar in Berlin. Mix this up with the fact there's table service, Budvar on draught and a decent grill menu with a soundtrack of Ellie Fitzgerald during the day, and the latest drum 'n' bass from New York in the evening.

RSVP

Edgar Buildings - 465777

Since being PJ's, some would say this place has gone downhill. The bar seems to be even more packed, the rooms seem to be even stuffier and the poten-

tially decent toilets don't seem to have had another loo roll delivery since. However, well decorated and with plenty of sofas if you can nab them, RSVP remains one of the first ports of call on most people's nights out, and during the day is a respectable place to unwind. Monday: double vodka Red Bull £3, Tuesday: House wine £5, Wednesday: 3 Rolling Rock's £5 and Thursday, two-for-one Bacardi Breezers. Sega Dreamcast available free of charge, non-smoking area and function room for hire.

Shades

4 Edgar Buildings - 466667

Right next to RSVP is Shades, an underground wine bar and restaurant. The low arched ceilings and candlelit tables make it the perfect place to get up to all kinds of jiggery-pokery. Also available for hire for your very own Shades party. The menu varies and food is served 12-2pm and 6-9pm, but the whole place closes in the afternoon. Tortilla wrap with goat's cheese and salad £4.95, wine from £9.90 a bottle without food.

The Slug and Lettuce

George Street - 337666

Situated on the ground floor of the recently renovated York Hotel, a previously crumbling edifice at the top of town, the interior decorators for this particular chain of pubs have done us proud. From the soft, squidgy sofas and armchairs in one corner, to the smoking room at the other, there is a decent sized bar in between, with the usual amount of strong continental lager and wines to choose from. There are DJ's from Thursday (courtesy of Po Na Na) through to Sunday with the customary laid-back vibes associated with any Sunday venue. The food is the usual high standard we've come to expect from the Slug chain.

Shades wine bar

Shades' gorgeous suntrapped garden available for hire this summer

FOOD

Lunch 12-2PM
Evening 6-9PM

Shades is available to hire for private parties all year round

4 Edgar Buildings. George Street. Bath
01225 466667

itchycities...

www.itchycity.co.uk

clubs

www.itchycity.co.uk

Babylon

Kingston Road - 400404

This club has changed that many times I've lost count, but now it's run by Karanga there's a reliable feeling about it, and you're safe in the knowledge you'll be hearing some quality sounds. A fairly youngish crowd keeps the bars busy as there are good drinks promotions happening all the time, and the club is only a short trip down the back stairs of Bar Karanga.

Cadillacs

90b Walcot Street - 464241

Cheesetastic nightspot in the true sense of the word. If you want to pull Sharon or Tracy, Darren or Wayne then this is where you should be heading. Identikit punters in a townie paradise. On the flip-side, however, this club does host quite a decent comedy club called the Fez. So if people ever ask you if you've been to 'Sadillacs' tell them you have but it was for the comedy, but then that could be a Saturday night anyway.

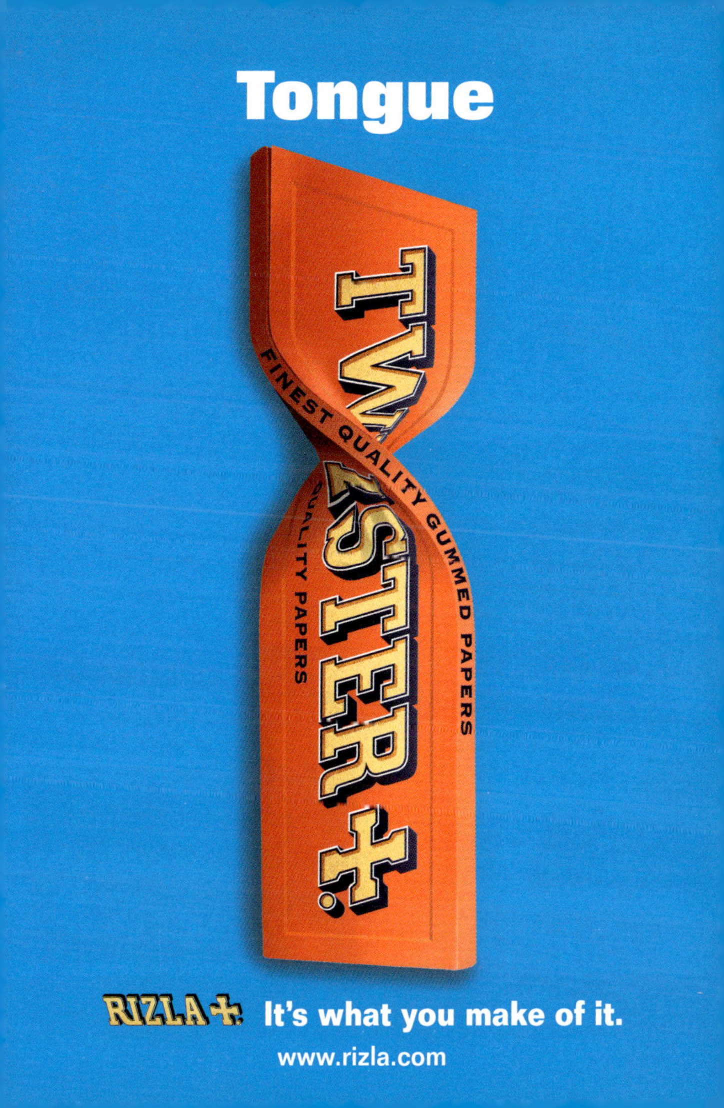
Tongue
TWISTER+
FINEST QUALITY GUMMED PAPERS
QUALITY PAPERS
RIZLA+ It's what you make of it.
www.rizla.com

The Fez Club

7a Bladud Buildings - 444162

Following on from the huge successes of the Po Na Na chain comes Bath's latest drinking spot. Not a club in the true sense of the word, but more of a place to relax and unwind at the end of the night, without the usual club pretence you get almost everywhere else. There are DJs most nights, and a dancefloor if you're that way inclined, but the intentions are for more of a drink than a dance. The door policy is strictly over 21 which should, with a bit of luck keep some of the young hoolies out.

TOP FIVE

Places to pull

1. **Cadillacs**
2. **T's**
3. **Baty's**
4. **Shades Wine Bar**
5. **Moles**

Moles

14 George Street - 404445

Intimate or cramped, cool or sweaty, this old lady (in comparison to many of the upstarts) of Bath nightlife will keep you entertained on whatever night you decide to step through the tiny entrance, but remember to mind your head as you walk in. Moles is one of those venues you talk about in a few years time and say to your mate next to you, "I saw them at Moles". I know, as I've bored people for years about seeing Oasis play about four songs before shouting at the small crowd and storming off. At least that's what I remember. A whole host of unheard bands have played here over the years including Blur, Mansun, Manics and Pulp. So get yourself down to see if you can spot an up-and-coming for yourself. There's a whole brewery full of real ales and lagers to be consumed in either of the two bars, but if you're standing through the walkway near the stage beware of people reaching behind you to put their empty pints on the shelf above your head, as they often miss. Life memberships are £15 and students get them for a fiver.

Po Na Na

The Basement

8/9 North Parade - 401115

One of the better examples in the Po Na

Hot tip

Na chain. Being set underground gives it a distinct cavernous feeling, but the décor has seen better days and could do with a bit of an upgrade. Then again, who gives a monkeys if the music's good and the drinks are flowing. Busy most nights during the week, but expect to queue for a long time at the weekends if you don't get there before pub kicking out time. If you pull there are loads of little hideaway places to go and snog away in.

Lucy
21
Student

Where do you go to show everyone just how funky you are?
Fez Club (on a Saturday)
And to mop up the excess alcohol?
Pasta Galore
I like your style. Where do you shop?
Gaff usually
What turns your taps in Bath?
Easy-going pace of life
And pulls your plugs?
Good clubs are hard to find

Savilles

Saville Row - 425550

One of those 'can't be arsed with a club but need more booze' type places - not so much a club as a late-night drinking place. Always popular, particularly at weekends. If you don't manage to get there before 11 when it's free entry. You'll have to get someone to sign you in as it reverts to a membership-only bar. Quite an intimate drinking den; if it weren't for the music seeping out onto the street you'd never guess what this place was, as the door's usually closed. You'll probably have to ring the bell to gain entry. Open until 2am.

T's Club

Spring Gardens Road - 425360

Another underground club, more in the physical sense than attitude; it isn't Cream, but then we are in Bath. Heavy on the students with its indie and dance anthems music policy. As with most clubs in the city the only sober people are the bouncers, and the bar staff, like everyone else, are quite happily off their trolleys. Completely unpretentious, good drinks deals and big fun (not the band, thankfully) for everyone.

RIZLA+ It's what you make of it.

Monday

Club/Bar	Night	Money	Drinks promos	Description
The Bell	Live bands	Free	-	Jazz orientated live music
The Fez Club	Groove	Free	-	Rare grooves & classics
Moles	Monday Live	Mem £2, conc. £2.50, guests £3		Local unsigned band night
Po Na Na	Love Lounge	Free	Dbl Vod R/Bull £2 B4 10.30	RnB-Big Beat-Breaks-House
Porter	Dip Dab	Free	NUS happy hour all night	Pick 'n' Mix of quality grooves

Tuesday

Club/Bar	Night	Money	Drinks promos	Description
Babylon	Fresh & Funky	£2 (£1 with flyer)	Dbl Vodka Red Bull £2	Swing, Hip Hop & RnB
The Fez Club	Burn	Free	-	Chilled Hip Hop & RnB
Hat & Feather	Film night	Free	-	Classics, cult & animation for your delectation
Home	Joan Davis & Friends	£5 (free with dinner res.)	-	Jazz Grooves
Moles	The Big Cheese	Mem £2, conc £2.50, guests £3	-	Cheap drinks and cheesy toons
Po Na Na	Glamourpuss	£2.50, £1.50 conc.	Dbl Vod R/Bull £2 B4 10.30	70's, 80's & 90's disco tunes
Porter	-	Free	-	Live band night

Wednesday

Club/Bar	Night	Money	Drinks promos	Description
Babylon	Incredible	£2 B4 10.30, £3 after, £2 NUS	Happy hour all night	Disco-funk-hiphop-house and soul
The Bell	Live bands	Free	-	Funk / Jazz / Folk live
The Fez Club	Loaded	£3	-	Big Breaks and Big Beats
Hat & Feather	DJ Derek	Free	Ska 'n' Jah	-
Home	Casa	Free	Latino	-
Moles	Mr Phats Funk Emp.	Mem £2, conc £2.50, guests £3	Dbl vodka £1.50 all night	Cruising instrumental jazz/funk
Po Na Na	Drive By	£2.50, £1.50 conc.	Dbl Vod R/Bull £2 B4 10.30	Bath's only DnB night with Garage once a month
Porter	-	Free	-	Various DJs

Thursday

Club/Bar	Night	Money	Drinks promos	Description
Babylon	Club Fusion	£3 B4 11, £4 after, £2 NUS	Happy hour all night	Alternative/Industrial/Mental Dance
Bar Karanga		Free	Stella bottles buy 2-4-1	Pre-bar for Saucy @ Po Na Na
Batys Bar	Salsa Mania	£4, £2.50 after 9.30	-	DJ Ruben's latin frenzy
The Fez Club	Sushi	£3	-	Mixed dishes by Natha & Pete B
Hat & Feather	Play Group	Free	-	Open mic and back line, free expression at its most rampant
Moles	Lost in the Mix	Mem £3, conc £3.50, guests £4	-	Live Indie bands on alternate thurs

Flick through the papers

Moles	Purr	Mem £3, conc £3.50, guests £4	-	-
Porter	-	Free	-	Live band night
Po Na Na	Saucy	£2, £1 conc.	Dbl Vod R/Bull £2 B4 10.30	Chilled sounds right thru to the latest in big beat, hip hop...

Friday

Babylon	Superfly	£3 B4 11, £5 after	Happy hour 9.30-11	70's Funk & Disco (open 'til 3)
Bar Karanga	Fresh 'n' Funky	Free	Stella bottles 3 4 £5	Hip Hop, Soul & RnB
The Fez Club	Deep	£3 B4 10.30, £5 after	-	Deep & jazzy grooves hosted by John Seaman, Steve Mulatto etc.
Hat & Feather	Petty Fraud Clinic	Free	-	Big beat & break beats from Kool Karl 'n' special guests
Litten Tree	Hot & Juicy	Free	-	Up tempo soul and dance
Moles	Elixir	Mem £3.50, conc £4, guests £4.50	-	Hip hop, beats, house
Porter	-	Free	-	Various d.j.'s
Po Na Na	Candy Floss	£2 B4 10, £5 after	House beer £1.50 B4 11	Cosmic House to Galactic Groove

Saturday

Babylon	Relentless	£4 B4 11, £5 after	Happy hour 9.30-11	Resident DJs (open 'til 3)
Bar Karanga	Free	-	Stella bottles buy 2 4 1	Pre-bar for Karanga @ Babylon
The Fez Club	Funk	£3 B4 10.30, £5 after	-	Classic funk, soul, reggae, house..
Hat & Feather	Live room	Free		Live sessions, today the Hat tomorrow the World!
Hat & Feather	Scorchio!	Free	-	Latin lowdown on the hispanic house highway
Moles	-	Mem £4, conc £4.50, guests £5	-	National bands
Porter	-	Free	-	Various d.j.'s
Po Na Na	-	£3 B4 10, £5 after	House beer £1.50 B4 10.30	Funky house & bangin' floostompers, not to be missed

Sunday

The Bell	Live bands (l/times)	Free	-	Folk/busking style/World/laidback live
Hat & Feather	Eat my Hat	Free	-	Deep, funky percussive house with Nathan plus the odd show stopping guest. Plus special live acts.
Home	Back in the Day	Free	-	Deli G (Galaxy 101)
Moles	Monday Live	Mem £2, conc £2.50, guests £3	-	Local unsigned band night
Porter	Comedy Cavern	Free	-	Comedy

RIZLA+ www.rizla.com

Walcot Street

There's a massively diverse selection of goodies to be had in this bohemian part of Bath. So if you start from town, you're offered the following from independent boutiques; hats, designer fridges, futons, fine cheese, mountain gear to old books, bikes and sewing machines. Then there's the flea market on Saturdays, where you can spend a good hour or so wandering from stall to stall bartering to get the right price. They even have their own passports on Walcot Nation Day when the whole street is given over to parades, music, food and a whole feast of other brilliant stuff. Watch out for this event as part of the Fringe festival in June.

Tai Tai Teahouse

51 Walcot Street - 01225 444122

Emperor Hui Tsun said that the tea leaves should be picked by young virgins with gold scissors. If this is how Tai Tai's

tea is picked, unfortuantely they don't have any video evidence. If your idea of a brew is limited to your gran's stewed pots then visit this serene temple of tea and you will be surprised at the different tastes on offer.

Shires Yard

A very classy indoor arcade in complete contrast to Walcot Street around the corner. If you've got time on your hands, amble through this lovely courtyard linking Milsom Street with Broad Street, gazing longingly at handmade chocolates, fine jewellery, Italian couture, the Alessi Gallery and other such finery. There are four food places as well, from sandwiches to excellent grub at the Moon and Sixpence restaurant.

The Podium Shopping Centre

Hot and busy shopping venue often just used as a walkthrough for people going to Waitrose, on their way to Pulteney Bridge or the library upstairs, but as in the rest of Bath, there are some good independent shops here. Art (Atrium Gallery), Beanie Babies (M.B.'s), books (Pumpkin), cameras (Walters), cushions (House Proud), gifts (Dickens & Dolphin), herbs (Julian Graves), juice (Riverside Juice Bar) and more.

Green Park Station

Green Park Road
Admin - 310418
Market - 789613

This splendidly restored Victorian railway station features a variety of specialist shops and stalls within the spectacular former train shed. The shops offer stationery and cards, picture framing, bags and belts, and men's hairdressing. Green Park Market runs Tuesday-Sunday, with the Bath Farmers Market (fresh local

Green Park Market at Green Park Station
Green Park Road, Bath

• Stationery and cards • Picture framing
• Bags and belts • Men's hairdressing

Monthly Art Exhibitions At Green Park Brasserie.
Free Friday Lunchtime Entertainment

Green Park Market runs Tuesday - Sunday, with the Bath Farmers Market on the 1st and 3rd Saturday of each month.

(Admin) 01225 310418 (Market) 01225 789613

produce and free entertainment) on the first and third Saturdays of each month. Watch out for 'Art at the Braz' - a rolling programme of art at Green Park Brasserie, 'Art in the Foyer', and 'Central Space Events'.

Department Stores

Jollys

7-14 Milsom Street - 01225 462811

Trading for over 165 years this big fancy department store now owned by House of Fraser is the ultimate in designer-label heaven. You can wander around in here for hours or just nip in and out as quickly as you can, avoiding Burberry-heavy tourists. Good bargains at sales time.

Rossiter's of Bath

38-41 Broad Street - 462227

An altogether different proposition than Jollys in that it's still an independent store owned and run by the family that gave the shop its name over 40 years ago. Sells all sorts of lovely housey things. Its veritable maze of an interior makes it feel very homely (windy, wooden staircases and little rooms) - an Aladdin's cave with something for every pocket.

Funky shops

Bloomsbury

15 New Bond Street - 461049

One of the better homeware shops in Bath for kitting out your pad that little bit differently. Full of funky bits, including stone statues and lovely electric fans that will turn any old semi into a palace fit for humans. Great reproduction Mackintosh chairs.

P.S. Bloomsbury also stocks the wonderful Neal's Yard range of remedies.

Stone the Crows

3 Broad Street - 460231

Great furniture/gift/joke/ceramics/clocks/fancy dress/kitchen sort of shop.

The Silly Fish Shoppe

6 Broad Street - 447353

Fishy plates, fishy cups, fishy picture hooks, fishy picture frames but no fish.

Tumi Latin American Gifts

8-9 New Bond Street Place - 446025

This fair trade shop has been established over 20 years and existed before everyone jumped on the ethnic handicraft bandwagon. The place for traditional, as well as bang up-to-date gifts from wind-chimes to rugs to music to furniture.

Gift shops

Paddington & Friends

1 Abbey Street - 463598

Tribute store to the little Peruvian bear with the big floppy hat and duffel coat, and a penchant for marmalade sandwiches. If they opened a café as well what would it sell, erm I wonder...

The Faerie Shop Ltd

6 Lower Borough Walls - 427773

Faerie stuff. Obviously. Nice little touches, the staff will add a sprinkling of 'faerie dust' to your purchase. A haven for girlies of any age.

Justice of Bath Ltd

16 Northumberland Place - 329300

Loads of unusual silver jewellery from designers such as Diana Porter, Sophie Harley, Rachel Simpson, Rita Lampen, Jess James, Jeremy Hoye to name but six. Belly bars, belly chains and toe rings sit amongst more standard types of jewellery. But all of it is worth spending that little bit more on. Some of the designers will work to commission as well if you have something a little more unusual in mind.

The Silver Gift Shop

25 Union Passage - 464781

Individual silver bits and bobs to decorate yourself and your house with.

Clothes - Men's

Green Room

26 Broad Street - 315444

Surf and snow boarding gear from the likes of Billabong, Rip Curl and AirWalk.

John Anthony

2 Quiet Street - 424066

One of those sort of shops you'd go to if you've got a family wedding coming up and you want to show everyone how well you're doing for yourself or you just like the finer things in life, like decent cut Italian suits. Two floors of Armani, Boss, Cerutti, Stone Island and Versace with shoes by Patrick Cox. Look out for bargains in the sales.

Kitchi Gai

28 Broad Street - 01225 465944

Good sized shop to wander round in and check out some decent branded, smart, casual clothes. Labels such as Sonetti, Duck and Cover, Urban Stone, Mish Mash and Gravity.

Route One

9 Broad Street - 446710

Quality street fashion/skate shop with all the usual labels as well as a fine selection of American gear. Clothes and skate shoes in the front of the shop and hardware (boards, blades and BMX) at the back.

Scallywag

3 York Street - 445040

Denim; Levi's, Lee, etc.

Westworld Clothing Co

36 Westgate Street - 447006

Busy and cramped or intimate depending how you look at it, but you'll find what you want amongst the rails. Classic streetwear from you know who brands - Carhartt, Porn Star, Addict as well as own label stuff, Bench, Hooch and WRC as well as AEM'KEI from New York.

TOP FIVE

Outside drinking

1. **Moon & Sixpence**
2. **Shades Wine Bar**
3. **Woods Restaurant**
4. **Crystal Palace**
5. **Café Rene**

Clothes - Women's

Apart from the usual chains such as Jigsaw, Karen Millen and Monsoon, Warehouse as well as upmarket clobber for the more mature lady there aren't many unique shops for the girls in Bath.

The Dressing Room

7 Quiet Street - 330563

Posh pants for ladies. The only lingerie shop in Bath; Dior, La Perla, Marie-Jo, Cotton Club, Aubade and Hanro.

Image

9 Shires Yard - 447359

Ready-to-wear designer clothing selling to a clientele aged 17 upwards, and if you're that age shopping here you must be pretty minted. Clothes by Max Mara, French label Macleod, Spanish label Amay Alzuaga. Shoes by Robert Clergerie, Luc Berjern and Paddy Campbell.

Square

5-6 Shires Yard - 464997

Upmarket with price tags to match. Designer labels including Ghost, Joseph & McQueen.

Unisex

Gaff

29 Upper Borough Walls - 448585

Streetwear from the likes of Diesel, Replay, Firetrap, Gas, Boxfresh etc.

Mayhem

6 Abbey Gate Street - 315001

Denim heaven. And I like it, I like it...

Maze Clothing

19 Green Street - 448201

Gorgeous, tactile clothes for men and women. Maze has its own excellent label plus Nicole Farhi, French Connection etc. Go on, bash that plastic and feel skint but fabulous!

NSJ Levi Store

5 Abbey Green - 463803

Guess? No, Levi's.

Zucci

7 Upper Borough Walls - 464392

The largest collection of suits in Bath. Only Bath stockists of Ted Baker along with Paul Smith and Kenzo suits and shoes with Ted Baker ladies as well as Sandwich and Sand. They also stock Canali suits direct from Milan, cheaper than you get them in Harrods, which inci-

JUSTICE

BRITISH DESIGNER JEWELLERY

THE DOGS BRACELETS

BATH
16 Northumberland Place
OXFORD
12 New Inn Hall Street
WINCHESTER
80 Parchment Street

0845 601 0751
WWW.JUSTICE.CO.UK

dentally is the only other place you'll get hold of them in the UK.

Footwear

All the main shoe companies (Bally, Clarks, Dolcis, Hush Puppies, K Shoes, Raw) are represented in Bath so you'll know you've a good chance of finding something you'll like. It's worth taking a look at the independent shops as well, but be prepared to pay.

Duo

33 Milsom Street - 01225 465533

Italian made shoes for women imported direct, mainly from the Florence area which is renowned for its leather. Also the odd Spanish and French shoes as well.

Jones Bootmakers

19 Cheap Street and 8 Green Street

Fine shoes at the upper end of the price market.

Mastershoe

92 Walcot Street - 460509

Huge shoe emporium in Walcot Street, where you'll find cheap shoes by the likes of Caterpillar, Doc's, Sketchers etc. They even have a welly section if you're that way inclined.

soletrader

9 Stall Street - 482040

Well stocked shoe chain in the heart of Bath's main shopping street. All the usual suspects on sale; Converse, Merrel, Cat etc.

Record/Music shops

Bath Compact Discs

11 Broad Street - 464766

Regarded as one of the country's finest independent classical record stores. Not being an expert, I couldn't vouch for it, but those in the know swear by it, which is good enough for me.

Duck Son & Pinker

9-12 Bridge Street - 466586

Musical instruments galore, anything and everything you can imagine.

HMV (UK) Ltd

13-15 Stall Street - 466681

Chart CD's, tapes, DVD, video, posters.

Nashers Music Store

72 Walcot Street - 332298

If you can't find anything that takes your fancy amongst 80,000 records in this temple of second-hand vinyl then you're deaf. Get those fingers dusty in amongst the racks or keep your fingers clean and check out their mail order section. Some rare finds to be had as well as a fair smattering of memorabilia. Like any second hand music store worth its salt, there are decks to try before you buy, but only if you can prise off the local DJs hunting for new tunes.

Onyx Music

7 The Corridor - 460945

Awkward sort of shop for finding what you want amongst the shelves. Loads of CDs but no vinyl.

Replay

27 Broad Street - 404060

Knowledgeable staff knocking out indie to dub reggae, taking on board all dance elements with a focus on drum 'n' bass. Good jazz and second hand selection, spread over two floors.

Subway Records

72 Walcot Street - 425376

Dance specialists. If you require house, hard house, hip hop or drum 'n' bass for your decks then check this basement of vinyl. You'll find all other aspects of dance covered including imports, promos and mix tapes in a chilled atmosphere. Friendly people.

Charity Shops

Worthy shopping is a good thing and you can't go wrong in Bath. All the usual shops throughout the city centre, as well as a fair smattering in student land, Oldfield Park. As Bath is a pretty wealthy city on the whole, there's a good chance that you'll find some pretty decent clobber at pretty decent prices.

Try the following:

City

Bath Women's Aid
70 Walcot Street, 424598

Imperial Cancer Research Fund
28 Westgate Street, 330570

Oxfam
12a George Street, 12 Argyle Street

Shaw Trust Charity Shop Ltd
11 George Street, 460225

Oldfield Park

British Red Cross Society
224 Moorland Road, 422561

Help the Aged
37 St Kildas Road, 447800

Shaw Trust Charity Shop Ltd
36 Moorland Road, 318764

Juan
21
Tourist

You look like you've been drinking. Where have you been?
Bath Tap

How about for a meal out?
Bella Pasta

Any shops in Bath match your 'zany' dress sense? Scallywag

Why Bath?
I love the buildings (yawn) and the people

Why not stay here for longer?
I have nowhere to stay!

CORKER

RIZLA + WARE

For the full Rizlaware range just visit www.rizla.com or call 07000 749527

If you're not fortunate enough to live here, on pages 60-62 we've mapped out a few ideas of how to maximise your stay:
- **2 hours**
- **24 hours**
- **Budget weekend in Bath**

Cinemas

ABC Cinemas
22 Westgate Street - 461730
Large cinema with approximately 600 seats, showing mainstream films which change fortnightly. Most big name films will play here first before retiring to one of the smaller, more intimate cinemas.
Adult - £4.60, Child & Concessions - £3.30

Little Theatre Cinema
St Michael's Place - 466822
Lovely little theatre catering for the more avant garde cinema-goer by showing independent, specialist and a small number of mainstream films.
Adult - £4.30, Child & Concessions - £3 (Except Bank Holidays)

Robins Cinemas
St John's Place - 461506
Another small cinema complex with three auditoriums of differing sizes. The largest of the three has around 200 seats, for the blockbusters, and the smallest has only 44 seats. Compact and bijou. Wonderful double seats at the back for snogging couples or singletons who want a bit more room.

Adult - £4.20, Child & Concessions - £3 (Fri/Sat all prices £4.20 after 5pm)

Theatres

The Rondo Theatre

Larkhall - 444003

Wonderful little theatre on the outskirts of Bath in the village of Larkhall. You get a feeling of belonging to a special club when you watch a play here, as the bar is right next to the seating, which is only a few feet from the stage. Everyone seems to know someone there and you can go and have a fag in the alleyway during the interval if it's too warm inside. I like the fact that you can take your beer or G&T to your seat and watch the performance. This theatre was originally a local concert hall which opened in 1989, but then received some well needed lottery dosh and re-opened in 1995 in the form you see it today. If you like your theatre informal but still with quality productions, then track this place down, especially during the fringe.

The Theatre Royal

Sawclose - 448815

This is one of the oldest working theatres in the country, built in 1805 and one which attracts many stars of stage and screen. Over the years the likes of Anthony Hopkins, Joan Collins, Charlton Heston, Glenda Jackson and even Olivier have played to packed houses. The theatre is no stranger to controversy, hosting Shopping and Fucking and God and Stephen Hawking before they appeared

on the West End. As part of the whole experience, there are two restaurants affiliated with the theatre, the Vaults Bar & Restaurant is a particularly fine example, as is the recently opened Prometheus Restaurant & Grill. You could alternatively hang out in the Garrick's Head before or after the show to try and catch a glimpse of one of the actors. In addition to the main house is the Ustinov Studio, built with a donation from the great man himself. This fringe theatre hosts a load of smaller plays and one-man shows, as well as theatre workshops for the kids.

Sport and Recreation

Bath City Football Club

Twerton Park - 313247

Lower division footy. Get behind your local team, even if you are only a 'local' for the weekend! Yes, that means you 'so-called' Manchester United fans, who've never even put your arse on a seat at Old Trafford.

Bath Cricket Club

North Parade Road - 425935

A great day out for all you cricket lovers. Typically 'British', with a wonderfully quaint tea house. In fact, the very same tea house was said to have floated away in 1859 owing to the Great Flood It's still there though, so work that one out.

Bath Racecourse

Lansdown - 424609

First class racing on the Lansdown hill. Always good for a day out. Buses run regularly from the bus station on race days.

Bath Rugby Club

The Recreation Ground - 325200

Top class Premiership and European Cup rugby action. If you're fed up not being able to sink a pint or two whilst watching the footy then get yourself to the rugby, where you can drink continuously throughout the game.

Bath Sports and Leisure Centre

North Parade Road - 462563

Swimming, squash, basketball, indoor footy, outdoor footy...usual leisure centre activities available.

Museums

American Museum

Claverton Manor - 460503

Open: End of Mar until late Oct

Tues-Sun: 2pm-6pm (closed Mondays except during August and Bank Holidays)

Bank Holiday Sunday and Monday: 11am-5pm

Limited openings for Christmas (18 Nov - 10 Dec)

Prices: Adults £5.50, Concessions £5, Child £3

This museum situated overlooking the valley of the River Avon houses an impressive collection of American Decorative Arts, and shows in detail the American way of life from 17th century colonial times up to the eve of the Civil War in the 19th. Each room is furnished authentically with a guide in each if you can't work out on your own what's happening. Every year the gardens put on a huge re-enactment of the Civil War, and

Brian
26
IT Support

Are you teetotal? No way! You can usually find me at The Star

Where do you practice your culinary seductions? Adventure Café

Funky clothes, eh. Where they from? Kitchi Gai

What keeps you chirpy in the mornings? Nothing

And what makes you lose the will to live? The sound of my bird whinging

if you've never seen one of these things it's worth checking out. Men and women dressed in weird clothes shooting blanks at each other may not sound fun, but when you see it all going off in different directions...well, go see for yourself.

Jane Austen Centre

40 Gay Street - 443000

Open:
10am until 5.30pm Mon-Sat
10.30 until 5.30pm Sun
Prices: Adult £3.95, Seniors & Students £2.95, Child £1.95
Family ticket £9.95 (2 adults and up to 4 children aged 16)

Following on from all the costume dramas that have flooded our TV screens over the last few years comes this museum dedicated to the person who's responsible for most of them being there in the first place. Regarded as Bath's celebrated authoress, despite the fact the woman allegedly despised living in the city (although not nearly as much as I despised studying her for my A-levels). There's an awful lot of material surrounding her stay. Basically an exploration of the life and times of the woman set in a Georgian townhouse.

Museum of Costume

Assembly Rooms - 477789

Opening hours:
Open 10am until 5pm daily all year (except 25/26 December)
Prices: Adult £4, Seniors £3.60, Child £2.90
Family ticket: £11 (2 adults and up to 4 children aged 16)
Joint ticket with Roman Baths included:
Adult £8.90, Seniors £8.00, Child £5.30

A sumptuous tour of all manner of clothes designs awaits the most dedicated followers of fashion. If you're into still life exhibits with fancy clothes dating back to Elizabethan times right through to contemporary designers such as Galliano, Armani and McQueen, then this is for you. All the clothes on display are original versions.

Included in the entrance fee you get a

www.itchybath.co.uk

tour 'wand' which are excellent guides to use. As well as this you get to see the Ballroom, Octagon, Tea Room and Card Room all part of the Assembly Rooms. The Georgian equivalent of having tea at the Ritz.

The Royal Photographic Society

The Octagon - 462841

Opening hours:

9.30am until 5.30pm daily all year (except 25/26 December)

Prices:

Adult £4, Seniors £2

Family ticket £8 (2 adults and 2 children up to age 16)

This museum is dedicated to the art of photography and has a permanent display of rare photographs and equipment. You can also take a look at the holography gallery and the constantly changing contemporary photographic exhibitions in the Octagon Galleries. Definitely worth a visit.

Roman Baths & Pump Room

Stall Street - 477785

Opening hours:

Daily all year (except 25/26 December)

October - March 9.30 - 5.00pm

April - September 9.00 - 6.00pm

August 9.00 - 6.00pm

Torchlit visits on August evenings 8.00 - 10.00pm

Prices:

Adult £6.90, Seniors £6,

Child (aged 6-18) £4

Family ticket £17.50 (2 adults and 4 children)

The Roman Baths are on the site of the UK's only natural hot spring, dating back 2000 years. This is where the Romans came to chill out when they'd had enough empiring for the day. In fact, according to the exhibition, it seemed as though they were the original loafers, lounging around all day in their togas chewing the fat with their pals down at the old spa. Ancient relics abound here in this excellent monument to Roman ingenuity and Georgian architecture. Set quite a bit of time aside for the visit as there are absolutely heaps of things for you to see here. From the ruins of the temple of Sulis Minerva (Romano-Celtic goddess of the springs) alongside treasures that were offered to her, classical temple carvings, inscriptions and sculptures revealing the lives of the Aquae Sulis people.

Sally Lunn's Refreshment House & Museum

4 North Parade Passage - 461634

A very popular destination for tourists and a place most locals will only visit when friends and family come to stay. Built in 1446 this is the oldest house in Bath and is also home to the Sally Lunn bun, which, just like Coca Cola, is still made to the original secret recipe from back in the day. As well as scoffing your face on buns you can also take a look at the kitchen museum which shows remains of Roman, Saxon and medieval buildings. Fascinating.

Activities

Ghost Walk

463618

Start time: 8pm at The Nash Bar, Garrick's Head
Finish time: Approx 10pm
Season: Mon - Sat (1st April - 31st Oct)
Fridays only (1st Nov - 31st March)
Prices: Adults £4. Children, Seniors and Students £3.00
A seriously wicked tour of Bath covering every haunted nook and cranny, including the infamous "Man in the Black Hat" amongst many others. Be afraid, be very afraid. In Bath no one hears you scream.

Avon Valley Cyclery

442442

Car park at the back of Bath Spa train station.
Opening hours: 9am-5.30pm
Types of bike: Mountain bike hybrids with detachable trailer bikes for kids
Price: £14 for a full day, £9 for a half day.
Bike hire for the active type of tourist. Bound only by your own energy, enthusiasm and time constraints you can go anywhere when hiring a bike from these guys. Most people, though, tend to pootle up and down the canal. Save your energy and head straight to the really good pub a few miles down in Bathwick, called the George Inn. Good for lazing about for a few hours in the sun beside the water. Dodgy for getting back after a few sherberts though.

Bath Boating Station

Forester Road - 466407

Opening hours: 10am-6pm
Seasons: Weather permitting, but usually from Easter until late September

Prices: Returnable deposit of £30, Adult £4.50, Child £2.25 1st hour, £1.50 each hour afterwards
Concessions: Students can hire boats for the day for £6
Traditional Thames skiffs and punts for lazy days on the river, or by prior arrangement you can book customised hours. I hired one overnight once and went for a midnight row up the river and watched the sun come up in beautiful countryside surroundings. There are 60 boats in total for hire, ranging in size up to a maximum of seven in a skiff, but in the summer months book at weekends to be on the safe side, though they will only hold the boat until midday. Take some Pimms, a picnic and have your own party in a punt.

TOP FIVE...

Tourist Attractions

1. **Roman Baths**
2. **American Museum**
3. **Building of Bath Museum**
4. **Bus Tour**
5. **Westonbirt Arboretum**

Days out

Westonbirt Arboretum

Tetbury, Gloucs - 880220

Opening hours: Open daily 10am - 8pm
Prices: Phone for details
18,000 trees (some over 170 yrs old), 600 acres of landscaped countryside, 17 miles of marked trails, leafy glades, giant redwoods etc etc. If taking yourself off for some proper relaxation is your thing, then beg, borrow or erm steal a car to get over to Westonbirt Arboretum. Any time of year is good, but autumn is probably the best time for running through huge piles of leaves like you were a kid again. Big thick cuddly sweaters, scarves and gloves and walks with your bitch.

Stonehenge

Off A303, Wiltshire - 01980 624715 (for crappy recorded message) or 623108 to speak to a real person

Opening hours: Varying between 9am and 7pm depending what time of year
Prices: Adults £4, concessions £3, Child £2 Family ticket £10 (2 adults & 3 children up to age 16)
Stone circle, big stone circle, druids, chanting, summer solstice. Quite a drive out of Bath, but you have to visit it really, don't you? The strange thing about Stonehenge is that it's just there, sitting quietly, minding its own business by the side of the A303 in Wiltshire. The really crappy thing is you can't go and touch the stones these days, and there's a depressing visitor centre and underground tunnel to negotiate before even getting near the place. Although 'Henge' is a must see place you could do worse than go visit Avebury stone circle for free, and though the stones aren't as big

THE INDEPENDENT The best coverage of news & sport

or impressive as 'Henge', Avebury is the biggest circle in the UK and it's free.

Glastonbury

Holy Grail, Isle of Avalon, King Arthur, Hippies, music festivals, naked dancing in the street. All of this can be found in Glastonbury, though the music festival held annually is actually held at Worthy Farm a few miles outside the village. For 30 years local residents have been raging about the noise of the music and 'wild-eyed druggies' wandering the village hassling the yokels with droogs, but it's not like that, honest. The festival is held at the end of June and is massive. Don't take my word for it, I've only been going for the last, how many years, oh I can't remember - it must be the droogs. Festival aside, the village of Glastonbury does have alot of hippies lingering on but now they're considered New Age and trendy with their crystals, Buddha statues, and whale music tapes. Lot's of little cafes, gift and bookshops to discover before hiking up Glastonbury Tor for magic views of the surrounding countryside. Legend has it that the Holy Grail is buried somewhere around here, and that there is a thorn tree growing in the grounds of the Abbey which has been there since Joseph of Aramathea stomped his staff into the ground on a visit to the place ages ago. So you can see there's loads to do, myths and legends abound in this medieval village.

Beckford Tower

Lansdown Road

460705 (weekdays) 422212 (weekends)

Opening hours (Weekends and summer Bank Holidays only)

10.30am - 5pm

Price: Adults £2.50, concessions £2, family £6

Situated up on Lansdown, above the city, this tower, which was built in 1827 by the very wealthy, eccentrically gay novelist, William Beckford, has recently been renovated (by my next door neighbour) so you can now climb to the top to see why he had it built. Fantastic views all around you, especially if you fancy popping in to Lansdown cemetery situated nearby.

Open Top Bus Tours

Guide Friday

444102

Price: Adults £8.50, Concessions £6.50, Child (5-12 years) £3.00

Family ticket (2 Adults & 4 Children) £20

Hop on, hop off bus tour with an English-only speaking guide on board, no other languages are available. The tour costs are quite expensive for a continuous one hour tour, but if you keep your ticket it gives you discounts on loads of other attractions in the city.

Bath Bus Company

330444

Price: Adults £6.50, Concessions £5.50. Another hop on, hop off bus company but with a taped continuous commentary in headphones in 7 different languages. The usual tourist sites are included.

Mad Max Tours

325900

Price: £15 (not including entrance fee to Stonehenge)

This independent tour company gives excellent value for money on its tour of Stonehenge, Avebury Stone Circles, Wiltshire White Horses, Lacock National Trust Village and Castle Combe. All are prime visitor attractions. The whole trip lasts nearly eight hours so it's quite full on, but definitely worth a go.

Two Hours in Bath

If you've only got a couple of hours to kill in Bath, then I suggest you get yourself onto one of the many open top bus tours. All pretty much the same except some have live commentary and some have headphones. This should take up about an hour if you don't get off. After that, head to the Roman Baths for an in-depth look at how the city got its name with a guided tour of the hot baths and Roman artefacts.

If the weather is pretty inclement and you just want to sample some of the city's atmosphere then there's no better place than the pub. There are some fine examples, all of which you can read about in this guide, but try The Crystal Palace or The Old Green Tree, which are both central and serve decent food.

24 Hours in Bath

Bear in mind that Bath is by no means a 24-hour city (a lot of stuff closes around 6 o'clock), and the time of day you arrive will determine what to do first. Here's a list of things that you shouldn't miss whilst in town...

Open top bus tour - you can get on and off at your leisure with these buses, so take time out to have a proper look at the Royal Crescent, Circus, Pulteney Bridge (3 hours)
Roman Baths (2 hours)
Walcot Street shops, Shires Yard shops, Podium, Green Park, Milsom Street, Broad Street - the list is long and it will take you a good afternoon to hike around the lot of them (4 hours)
Pubs - there are loads of 'em, high street chain pubs to ickle indie backstreet pubs (4 hours)

Budget weekend

Firstly, get yourself booked into the Bath Backpackers Hostel. It's cheap, clean and very friendly, though you won't get an en-suite shower.
If you were to arrive on a Friday night, leaving mid-afternoon on Sunday then follow the list below to experience the good, the good and some of the ugly - there should never be any badness.

Friday Night

Drinking - obviously your first priority on a Friday is to check out some good bars, a club and a good takeaway. You're scr-wed on the club front so opt for a meal instead and save your moves 'til tomor-row night. As there's a serious lack of clubs to choose from you could probably take in dinner on the Friday, and take in a couple of clubs on the Saturday night.

Beer prices obviously vary from pub to pub. Generally prices are about £2.50 a pint these days, but you'll find cheap deals in some venues. Classic Friday action can usually be found in Lambrettas Bar, the Hat & Feather or at the top end of Milsom Street, where you can choose from Litten Tree, RSVP, Baty's or Slug & Lettuce.

After you've trawled the bars you've got a choice of Cadillacs, Moles, Po Na Na or T's for your clubbing or The Huntsman and Savilles for late-night drinking action. Where you end up will determine which takeaway you eat. After Cadillacs you could go for a Schwartz burger, after Moles head towards the chicken shop on Monmouth Street. After Po Na Na and T's there's Marmaris for a kebab.

After you've woken up with a hangover, head to Lovejoys in the Bartlett Street antiques market for a decent fry up. When you've bolted your bacon, slope off to the flea market on Walcot Street where there's loads of stalls to browse around.

Saturday is when the world and his wife go shopping, and if you're up for it, why not join in? There's heaps of shops to keep you going for hours on end, and enough time to do some serious damage to your plastic. A spot of retail therapy usually sorts out a good hangover and builds up an appetite. If the hair of the dog is in order, try a leisurely lunch in one of Bath's numerous restaurants before heading back out onto the streets.

It's probably about now that you should start thinking about getting some culture inside you, for which Bath is quite rightly famed. As Saturday's are usually pretty damn busy it's not a good time to take an open top bus tour. Save that for Sunday morning when you've got zero energy and the streets aren't as busy. If you need to get away from the bustle, go and have a wander around inside the Abbey before crossing over the churchyard and into the Roman Baths.

All this should set you up nicely for a bit of a kip before heading out for more drinking, but beware, Saturday night is townie night. You'll see them everywhere you go and it'll be hard to avoid them, so just watch your step. Again, the same rules apply on the club side on a Saturday as they do for Friday. I'm afraid there isn't much choice.

After a leisurely breakfast on Sunday morning, take the bus tour, which you can, hop on or off at any of the designated points. This should round up your weekend nicely.

Accommodation - £30 double room
Club entry (2 nights) - approx £10
Bath Abbey - free - but they press you for a donation
Roman Baths - £6.90 - free to residents so try and blag it
Bus tour - £6.50
Total - £53.40 plus your booze and grub.

carrots aren't blue...

and shares aren't free

But we'll give you 1000 free shares in BlueCarrots when you join the growing community of BlueCarrots members who enjoy CashBack from a huge range of famous online stores. No catches, just CashBack.

BOL 7% CashBack
Electrical Warehouse 6% CashBack
Firebox 6% CashBack
Games and Videos 5% CashBack
Into Fashion 5% CashBack
Mad About Wine 5% CashBack
Magazine Shop 5% CashBack
Think Natural 5% CashBack
Kitbag 4% CashBack
Charles Tyrwhitt 5% CashBack

BlueCarrots.com
CashBack EVERY TIME you shop

SHOPSAFE™

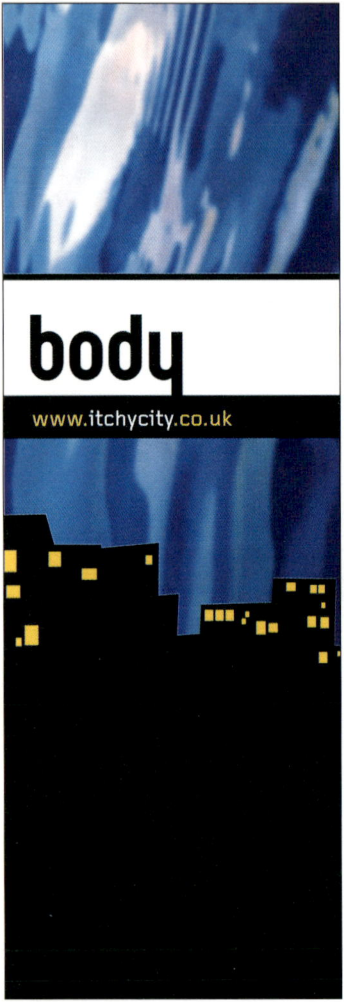

Hairdressers

Artizan Hair

8a George Street - 447087

Opening hours:
8.45am - 5.30pm (Mon-Fri)
8.30am - 4.00pm (Sat)
Ave. men's cut: £19
Ave. women's cut: £23
Concessions: 10% on cuts only (Mon -Thu)

Very friendly, helpful salon with a good reputation.

Hacketts

Green Park Station - 465200

Opening hours:
9.00am - 6pm (Mon & Tues)
9.00am - 8pm (Wed & Thu)
9.00am - 6pm (Fri)
8.30am - 5pm (Sat)
10.00am - 4pm (Sun)
Ave. cut: £15
Wet shave: £12.50
Concessions: 10% for students anytime
Seniors specials 9am - 12am (Mon-Fri)
Specialist cuts? Anything goes
If ever a salon could be called opulent then I suppose this would be it. Opened three years ago as part of the re-gener-

ation of the old Green Park station this men only salon is elegantly furnished with proper barbers chairs for that authentic feel, but certainly not like that Saturday morning feeling when you were a kid.

Factory Hairdressing

10 Julian Road - 465620

Opening hours: 10am until late
Ave. men's cut: £18
Ave. women's cut: £23
Concessions: Student discounts (M-Th)
Specialist cuts? Told me they do dreads but my girlfriend reckons you can do them yourself! But she's dead clever like that. With each hairdresser working for themselves in this laid back comfortable salon. There's no real closing time apart from when they want to go down the pub. You get a really good cut here. Recommended.

Toni & Guy

2 New Bond Street - 484284

Opening hours:
9am - 7pm (M-F)
9am - 6pm (Sat)
10am - 4pm (Sun)
Ave men's cut: £25
Ave women's cut: £40
Concessions: Student cuts £20 men, £25 women
Usual Toni & Guy efficiency but ask to be seated upstairs where it's more comfortable rather than the manic treadmill below.

Nick Brain

15 York Street - 462676

Opening hours:
9am - 5.30 (M-W & Sat)
9am - 6.30 (Th-Fr) or late depending on stylist
Ave. men's cut: £20
Ave. women's cut: £30
Concessions: Student discounts are available depending on the stylist
Specialist cuts? 2 colour technicians and 2 long hair specialists (does that mean they're hippies?)

Well respected and recommended stylists.

The Forge Hairdressing

11 Beaufort Square - 01225 484888

Opening hours: 9am - 6pm (Tues-Sat)
Ave. men's cut: £18
Ave. women's cut: £28
Concessions: None

Stylish hairdressers tucked away behind the Theatre Royal.

TOP FIVE...

Places for Stag/Hen dos

1. Cadillacs
2. Litten Tree
3. RSVP
4. Slug & Lettuce
5. Baty's

Address http://www.itchybath.co.uk Go

Health Clubs

Kings Health Club

Avon Street - 461111

Opening hours: Mon-Fri: 7am - 9.30pm
Sat & Sun: 8.30am - 4pm
Membership: £95 joining fee (paid once)
Monthly charge £22.50
Concessions: Initial joining fee (paid once) £45
Monthly charge £18.50

A really friendly gym. Tailor made programmes for people of all shapes and sizes, so there's no pressure to join those classes full of Posh 'n' Becks look-alikes. A good sized selection of classes are available, as well as a big selection of machines to work out on. This converted college theatre is light, airy and open plan. Too many mirrors on the exercise floor allow you to look at yourself red faced, and drenched in sweat. But overall it has a good reputation.

Living Well Health Club

Walcot Street - 310061

Opening hours: Mon-Fri: 7am - 10pm (off peak Mon-Fri: 9am - 5pm)
Sat & Sun: 8am - 9pm
Membership: Gold Individual (unlimited usage) £100 joining fee
Monthly charge £30
Off peak Individual £75 joining fee
Monthly charge £20

Very professionally run gym part of the huge Living Well health club chain on the second floor of the Hilton hotel. Just a small amount of machines to use though they do run tailor made programs. It has a pool, well, more of a pond really, Olympic size for the vertically challenged. Complimentary towels and toiletries thrown in, which can save a trip down to Boots.

Trim Street Trainers

7 Trim Street - 445027

Opening hours: 9am-8pm
Membership: £60 gym or class only
£75 combined (both annual fees)
Price per class: £3.50 non member
Concessions: Phone for details

At the time of writing this gym was undergoing a refit. A gym based more around office workers who don't want

THE INDEPENDENT ON SUNDAY The best writers, the sharpest opinions

to pay huge membership fees for a place they hardly ever go to. You basically pay for the class each time you go, though obviously the prices are cheaper if you are a member. Not the largest gym in the city but reasonably well equipped.

Sereen
23
Radio Production Assistant

Where do you go for a tipple?
Tilley's Bistro
And for the odd meal out?
Wok Wok usually does the trick
Expensive looking clothes – are they from round here? Actually, from Bristol
What turns you on?
Summer-time drinking on the boats
And what switches you off?
Townies, 'avin it large' on a Saturday night

YMCA
International House
Broad Street Place - 460471
Opening hours: Mon-Fri: 7am - 10pm
Sat & Sun: 8.30am 7pm
Membership: £50 joining fee (one off)
Monthly charge £20, classes £2 members, £3 non
Concessions: 50% off joining fee, monthly charge remains the same
On a par in terms of equipment with the rest of the health clubs in the city, with some very friendly and helpful staff. As part of the membership you get the usual appraisal (which is when you find out exactly how unhealthy and fat you are), exercise programme and ongoing assessment. There's also a health suite with sauna, steam and sunbeds for when you aren't sweating enough from one of the exercise programs in the sports hall.

Tattoos & Body Piercing

Unfortunately you have only one option for self mutilation (or body art, depending on how you look at it).

Bath Body Piercing Centre
24 The Vineyards - 463707
Prices vary depending on what you want done. Always very busy, especially Saturdays so try during the week.

Get cheap meal offers sent to your phone.
wap.itchycity.co.uk

Sarnies

Fodders

9 Cheap Street - 462165

Fancy sandwiches for office workers who can't be bothered making their own.

Take Five

Grove Street - 425888

Deadlines to meet, Richard and Judy to watch there are oh so many reasons not to visit the restaurant itself, so order a sarnie. Above average sandwich shop delivering up hot roast meat sandwiches, fresh tuna (not tinned stuff) and huge salad boxes. Bistro sandwiches. Could be a new thing?

Hardy's Café

14a Westgate Buildings - 316796

Biggest and best bacon butties in town. They're probably a little more expensive than most sandwich shops in town, but by golly they're good sized portions. If your hangover is kingsize and your appetite is the same then you've just gotta have the breakfast baguette. A whopping 2 eggs, 3 sausages and 3 rashers of bacon on a baguette will set you back 5p short of £3. Gutbustingly good.

Phipps Bakeries

3 Argyle Street, 4 George Street, 5 Orange Grove, 68 Lower Bristol Road

If you feel a pie munch coming on then I suggest you look no further than any of

the four Phipps bakery shops. Lancashire Hot Pot pie and roast chicken pie are all guaranteed tummy fillers. Beware, though, you might feel one isn't enough, two certainly is and three is just plain greedy, but they're that good. Favoured by the rugby crowd on a Saturday afternoon to soak up the Ushers and Guinness.

Montgomery's

10a Queen Street - 338803

Bloody good butties made fresh to order. A good all-round selection of fillings to stuff your baguette with before taking it to nearby Queen Square to sit in the sunshine.

Devon Savouries

19 Lower Borough Walls

Giant chicken 'n' sweetcorn please.

Kebabs, Burgers

Marmaris

4/5 Grand Parade - 461946

Best kebabs in town and always rammed at the end of the night. Eat in or take away.

Schwartz Bros

4 Sawclose - 461726

102 Walcot Street - 463613

Number one for your burgers in Bath. Forget the golden arches, this is where burgers begin and end. You cannot go wrong with a Schwartz burger. 'Nuff said.

Indian

Moghul Indian Takeaway

140 Walcot Street - 464956

The inhabitants of Walcot Street don't know how lucky they are to have this excellent curry shop on their doorsteps.

Ruposhi Indian Takeaway

3 Sussex Place

Widcombe - 337294

Why oh why don't you deliver Ruposhi? Superior curries for the Widcombe environs. Phone order your grub, walk to the offie, get your booze then collect your curry. Job done.

Fish n Chips

Ancient Mariner

8 Moorland Road

Oldfield Park

Good chips

THE INDEPENDENT www.independent.co.uk

It's 1:30 am. Where can I get a drink... with trainers on?
What time does that restaurant stop serving tonight?
I'm skint. Are there any happy hours at the moment?
Are there any decent garage nights on tonight?
Where am I going to find a wig for that 70's do tomorrow?
All your questions answered
at www.itchybath.co.uk

Yummy

Avon Fish Bar

2 Lambridge Buildings
Larkhall - 316664

Good chips, great curries. If you're in the vicinity of Larkhall village you have to checkout this chippy/curry shop as it's highly recommended.

Seafood

38 Kingsmead Street - 465190

Not exactly service with a smile, but what do you want when the chippers are fat and the fish is fried just right. Be posh and eat in to get your grub served on a plate.

Chinese

Cheong Sing Takeaway

26 Moorland Road
Oldfield Park - 337117

Chicken

Southern Fried Chicken

41 Monmouth Street - 462121

3 pieces of chicken, 2 ribs and chips please. Messy food but good honest grub when you feel the caveman instinct coming on. Best chicken shop in town.

Pizza

Pizza Kitchen

1 Wellsway
Bear Flat - 429776

Slightly on the expensive side for delivery pizza so walk there you lazy sods and get it cheaper over the counter. It does good burgers as well.

Il Bottelino

5 Bladud Buildings - 464861

Giant traditional thin crust Italian pizzas to either takeaway (restaurant hours) or eat in.

You can also find various mobile vans around the city at kicking out time, but usually they're at the Abbey taxi rank, and to be quite honest, they're crap.

TOP FIVE...

Cheap Eats

1. Il Bottelino
2. Pig & Fiddle
3. The Porter
4. The Green Tree
5. Adventure Cafe

find places for late drinks on your WAP phone
wap.itchycity.co.uk

accommodation

www.itchycity.co.uk

In the larger or more expensive hotels prices tend to vary depending on the time of year, so if you're not sure when you'll be staying it can be quite an achievement getting a price from them. There are many hotels, guesthouses and B&B's available all over the city, so here's just a brief summary of the good, the bad and the ugly.

All prices include breakfast.

Expensive

Bath Spa Hotel

Sydney Road - 444424

From £153 during the week and £105 at the weekend

Francis Hotel

Queens Square - 424257

From £121 during the week and £54 at the weekend

Hilton National

Walcot Street - 463411

From £95 during the week and £70 at the weekend (with use of the pool, sauna, gym etc, thrown into the price). All rooms have satellite TV.

Hey Baby, what's your Hotmail address?

Isn't it time to change your chat up line?

With MSN® Hotmail® whoever you pull can instantly go into your little black online book. What's more you can access your email any time, from any internet enabled PC – and your account is free. Don't miss out – visit *www.studenthotmail.co.uk* now and get your own personal email account.

email me ______ @Hotmail

Microsoft

Where do you want to go today?

Microsoft, the Microsoft logo, 'Where do you want to go today?', MSN, the MSN butterfly device and Hotmail are either registered trademarks or trademarks of Microsoft Corporation in the US and/or other countries.

msn™ Hotmail®

BATH BACKPACKERS HOSTEL

13 PIERREPONT STREET, BATH, BA1 1LA

While visiting bath come stay at the coolest budget hotel in Bath.
We are situated 30 metres from Bath's bus and train station and located right in the centre of Bath's pubs and clubs!!
We have private rooms, dormitory rooms, kitchen facilities, bar, pool room, internet access, free tea and coffee and hot showers.
Left luggage facility, guided pub-crawls and bookings for Stonehenge tours.

Book now on 01225 446787 or e-mail us on: stayinbath@backpackers-uk.demon.co.uk

Queensberry Hotel

Russell Street - 447928

From £135 all week rising to £185. All costs are per room not per person and are inclusive of continental breakfast, not English. The most expensive rooms are elegant 1st floor Georgian drawing rooms. Very tasteful with a fabulous restaurant in the basement.

Mid Price

Harington's Hotel

Queen Street - 461728

From £65 (Sun - Thurs) and £54 (Fri & Sat). All rooms have satellite TV.

Pulteney Hotel

Pulteney Road - 460991

From £45 during the week and £48 at the weekend.

The Royal Hotel

Manvers Street - 463134

From £47.50 during the week and £41 at the weekend. All rooms have satellite TV.

Sydney Gardens Hotel

Sydney Road - 464818

From £59 (Sun - Thurs) and £75 (Fri & Sat).

Budget

Only three budget hostels at the moment available in Bath, which is pretty poor considering the number of young people the city attracts.

Bath Backpackers Hostel

13 Pierrepont Street (5 mins walk from train station) - 446787

Friendly Aussie run hostel which requires a valid passport to stay. Dorms are £12 (a double will set you back £30) and need to be booked in advance. Lively and busy with the following extras on offer: kitchen facilities, satellite TV, internet access, pool room, late night bar (but watch your head on the way in), laundry and hot showers. A big bonus is that there is no curfew and no lockout. You can book Stonehenge tours from here with Mad Max, and this summer they have started to organise water skiing tours, and depending on their success will continue to do so.

Bath Youth Hostel (Y.H.A.)

Bathwick Hill - 465674

Dorms are £10.85 per night, twin rooms available at £30 with en suite at £35, 4 bed dorms with en suite are £55. There is no curfew but sadly the hostel doesn't have its own bar, but it is on the main student bus route out of the city which runs late services.

YMCA

Broad Street Place - 460471

Good, honest and cheap. Dorms are £11 (10 per dorm) or splash a further £4 on top to bag a single room. No curfew, but usual restrictions apply when it comes to alcohol. None allowed on the premises. You can use the gym if you want whilst you're there as well.

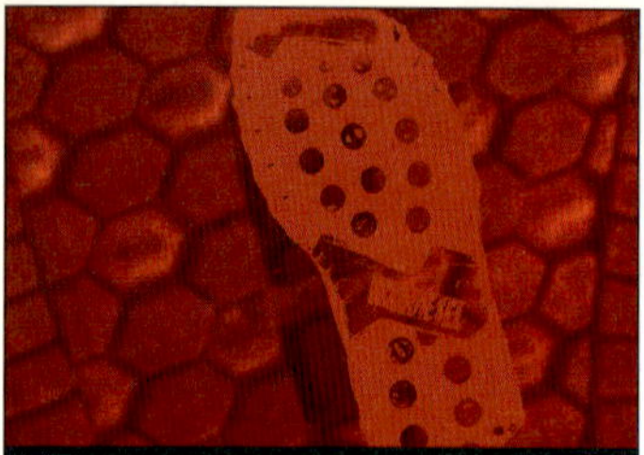

getting about & maps

www.itchycity.co.uk

Taxis and Private Hire

Abbey Radio Taxis
444444 or 444446

Coronation Cars
331298

Orange Grove Taxis
331298 or 447777

Rainbow Taxis
460606

Twerton Cab Service
444441

Widcombe Private Hire
422610

Limousines

American Stretch Limousines
709635

Fancy yourself as a bit of a flash git do ya? Top quality, fully licensed stretch Lincolns seating a maximum of 8 people get you there cosseted in leather, with TV, video and CD luxury. A couple of bottles of bubbly thrown in for good measure. £95 inc VAT for the first hour and then you can arrange a price with them individually.

Chauffeur Link
446936

More of the above for a minimum charge of £90 per hour, though jobs can be individually priced. So if you got a first in your finals and want to turn up at your graduation looking the star that you are, get your parents to stump some extra readies.

Buses

Bath Bus Company (local)
330444

First Badgerline (local)
464446

Includes Park 'n' Ride schemes @ £1.40 return, every 15 mins from 7.30 am.

National Express
0990 80 80 80

Trains

First Great Western
08457 000 125

National Rail Enquiries
0345 48 49 50

Planes

Bristol International Airport
01275 474444

Car Hire - Self Drive

Avis
446680

Ford Rent-a-Car
402234

National Car Rental
481898

FIND THE NEAREST CASHPOINT ON YOUR WAP PHONE
wap.itchycity.co.uk

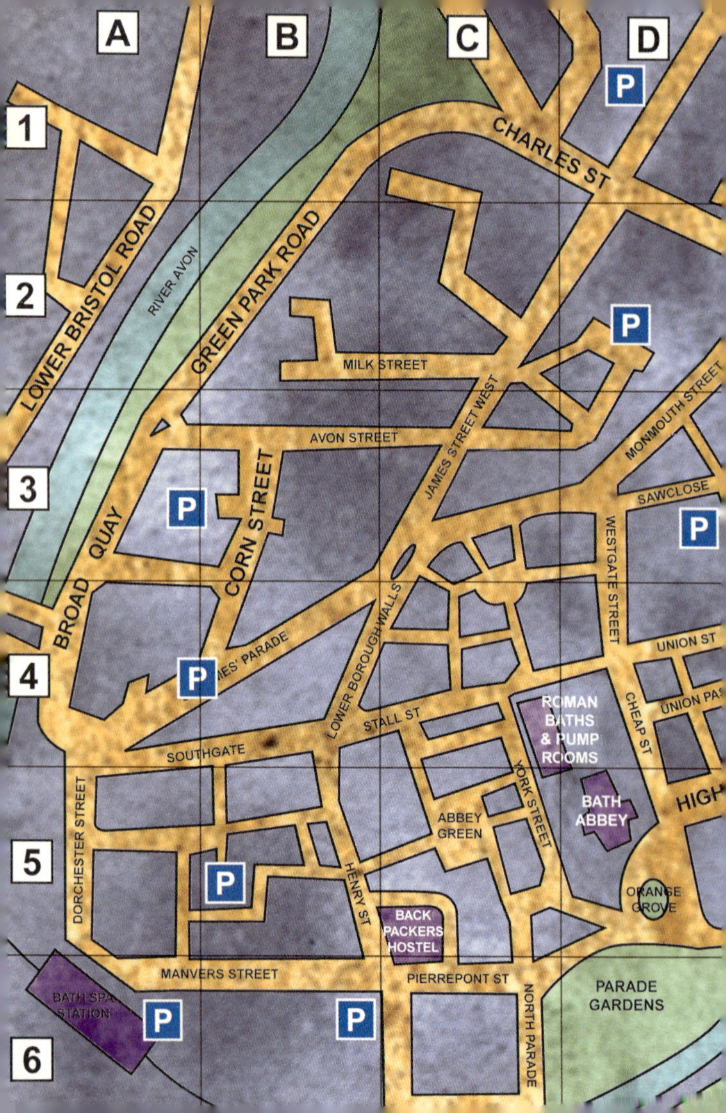
A
B
C
D
1
2
3
4
5
6
P
CHARLES ST
LOWER BRISTOL ROAD
RIVER AVON
GREEN PARK ROAD
MILK STREET
JAMES STREET WEST
AVON STREET
MONMOUTH STREET
SAWCLOSE
CORN STREET
BROAD
QUAY
WESTGATE STREET
UNION ST
UNION PAS
LOWER BOROUGH WALLS
STALL ST
ROMAN
BATHS
& PUMP
ROOMS
CHEAP ST
SOUTHGATE
YORK STREET
BATH
ABBEY
HIGH
ABBEY
GREEN
DORCHESTER STREET
HENRY ST
ORANGE
GROVE
BACK
PACKERS
HOSTEL
MANVERS STREET
PIERREPONT ST
NORTH PARADE
PARADE
GARDENS
BATH SPA
STATION